A Passage to Nuristan

A PASSAGE TO
NURISTAN

Exploring the Mysterious
Afghan Hinterland

Nicholas Barrington
Joseph T. Kendrick
Reinhard Schlagintweit

Foreword by Sandy Gall

I.B. TAURIS
LONDON · NEW YORK

Published in 2006 by I.B.Tauris & Co Ltd
6 Salem Road, London W2 4BU
175 Fifth Avenue, New York NY 10010
www.ibtauris.com

In the United States and Canada distributed by Palgrave Macmillan,
a division of St. Martin's Press, 175 Fifth Avenue, New York NY 10010

ISBN 1 84511 175 3
EAN 978 1 84511 175 5

A full CIP record for this book is available from the British Library
A full CIP record for this book is available from the Library of Congress
Library of Congress catalog card: available

Typeset in Sabon by Dexter Haven Associates Ltd, London
Printed and bound in Great Britain by MPG Books Ltd, Bodmin

Contents

Acknowledgements

The authors are grateful to Olaf Høeg (Kendrick's cousin in the United Kingdom) for his diplomatic coordination, his tireless persistence and his dedication to detail, which ensured that the book reached its final form. Also, to Ralph Helwig of Economic Strategies in the United States for his expert technical assistance, his problem-solving creativity and, above all, for his consistently positive approach. Nicholas Barrington is grateful to Deirdre Lay and Lesley Lambert for their typing, and to Sara Symes for the dagger photograph.

Reinhard Schlagintweit furnished the black and white photographs. The colour photographs came from the collections of Nicholas Barrington and Joseph T. Kendrick.

Any proceeds from this book, for the authors, over the cost of production, will go to UNICEF's work in Afghanistan.

Foreword

Nuristan is the remotest and least explored part of Afghanistan apart from the Wakhan Corridor, which pokes its finger into China. But whereas the very name of Nuristan carries with it a wealth of ancient culture and distant lore, the Wakhan, although magnificent scenically, lacks – for me, at any rate – the same romantic appeal.

I first visited the Land of Light in 1982, travelling from the Panjshir Valley south-east through Nuristan to Chitral, and found it an absorbing and spectacular experience. I repeated the journey, south to north and back again, four years later, in 1986. My travels, unlike those of the three diplomats chronicled in *A Passage to Nuristan*, were occasioned by the Russian invasion of 1979 to 1989. Having walked to the Panjshir by an easier but still arduous route, we were told by Ahmed Shah Masud, the guerrilla leader we had come to film, that it would be too dangerous to return the same way. We might be waylaid by his enemies and our film destroyed – clearly an unacceptable risk. Instead, he said, we had to go through Nuristan, which was already his main convoy trail.

So, in October 1982, accompanied only by two Panjshiri horsemen, a young Frenchman who spoke excellent Farsi and eight horses, we completed the journey in 12 days, crossing five high passes – Chamar, Kantiwar, Mum, Papruk and Peshawarak. On Papruk, which was very icy at the top, we got over only with the help of a score of tough Badakhshani mujahideen going to Chitral to collect weapons. In 1986 we found that the war was having an increasing effect. In Barg-i-Matal, for example, a small group of moneyed Wahabi Arabs had taken over the village, stopping and quizzing us aggressively, to the fury of our Panjshiri escort, Masud Khalili. Although many Nuristanis remained open and hospitable, others were distinctly unfriendly. One night, having camped outside a village, an angry old lady stoned us for helping ourselves to her hillside grazing. She was an excellent shot, hitting several horses. The mujahideen just laughed and moved away, but the intrusion of so many outsiders was undoubtedly resented.

I much enjoyed this fascinating book, which conveys the flavour and beauty of a very special part of Afghanistan. In word and picture, it captures the Shangri-La quality that still permeated Nuristan as late as 1960, when the authors made their visit – and which was still evident even in the 1980s. The fact that it must inevitably be eroded is what gives *A Passage to Nuristan* its poignancy and its appeal.

Their descriptions of the landscape are as charming as its flowering meadows and ice-cold rivers, in which one hardy member of the trio liked to bathe up to three times a day; as spectacular as the majestic mountain ranges; and as exciting as the traverse of a sheer rock face above a fast-flowing river. Most memorable of all, however, are their encounters with Nuristani tribes such as the Presuns, whose archaic language was spoken in only five or six villages and where all the men could have passed for cousins of the Seven Dwarfs. Indeed, one of their maleks looked exactly like Sleepy.

In such an idyllic account, one would have hoped for Snow White to complete the magic, but it was not to be. They did catch tantalising glimpses of the legendary beauty of the Nuristani women, but never face to face, and they were hardly ever able to capture it on film. Since the conversion to Islam of the Nuristani Kafirs, although comparatively recent, is now relatively complete, it seems we never will know what she really looked like. Perhaps it does not matter: Nuristan is the real heroine.

Sandy Gall

Preface

Over forty years ago, in 1960, we were three young diplomats and friends from the embassies in Kabul of Germany, Britain and the United States, who ventured into a virtually unknown region of Afghanistan, known today as Nuristan (Land of Light), formerly Kafiristan (Land of Unbelievers, Infidels), inhabited by an ancient people. This was an adventurous, one might say foolhardy, expedition, tolerated rather than encouraged by our respective ambassadors. There was little pressure of other work. The journey turned out to be one of the first to penetrate the region in the period after World War II, and it provided one of the few recorded observations of central Nuristan since the early 1890s, when the first pioneering westerner had visited and studied the Kafirs.

The 1960s in Afghanistan were a time in which the then King and his cousin, the Prime Minister (Sardar Daoud), through a benevolent if autocratic administration, were reaching out to bring their country out of the Middle Ages and into the modern world. Such an attitude and policy were met by an active response from outside powers. But the motivation of the two main powers – the United States and Soviet Union – were mixed: they were concerned with humanitarian development, but involved, in a sort of replay of the 'Great Game' of the previous century, in seeking to acquire influence in what was still a buffer state. Since the independence of Pakistan and India the British role had been taken over by the United States, the prime Western power. High-profile visits to Kabul were made both by President Eisenhower and Chairman Khrushchev. Each side was spying on the other.

The USSR was in expansionist mood. A Soviet threat to South Asia and a drive for commercial access to warm-water ports could not be discounted. The Soviet government was building roads in the northern sector of the country, exploring for oil and, above all, concentrating on building up the Afghan military establishment and exercising influence over it. The United States, operating largely in the southern reaches of the country, was likewise building roads, dams and a major airport (Kandahar), and in particular was trying to build up local educational institutions. Other Western countries were contributing in their own way. The government of Daoud was playing off one side against the other, but his nationalist policy of advocating a greater Pushtunistan alienated Pakistan and her Western friends. His people argued that Afghans sent for training in the Soviet Union, especially from the armed forces, would – as good Muslims – never become Communists. This turned out to be a tragic misjudgement.

Meanwhile, there were hundreds of foreigners in the country, mostly in Kabul, where the social life was active, as is often the case in remoter posts without entertainment facilities. They were resigned to having been sent to a backwater, virtually ignored by those at home, and largely confined to their small compounds. Most had little interest in the country around them. With few exceptions, even the staffs of the various embassies did not have many Afghan friends nor show much interest in the people, the culture or countryside, outside the incestuous social activities in Kabul and the specific projects on which they were engaged. Few could speak the local languages.

On the other hand, the three of us, young diplomats, got on well together because we were interested in all aspects of the local social culture: the people; the countryside, with its magnificent scenery and its obscure corners; and the relics of the country's rich history. Technically we were political officers, and we were particularly interested to take what opportunities we could to explore what was a largely unknown country. We liked Afghanistan, and its people – many of whom had never seen a foreigner but who were invariably hospitable and friendly. Any reports written at the time had minimal political content, and were relegated in capitals to the deep archives, forgotten about and not even utilised in the days ahead when the culture and sociology of the Afghans became a matter of international interest. In those days no one would have foreseen that, at the beginning of the next millennium, the eyes of the world would be focused on Afghanistan.

Against this background, with areas of the country gradually opening up, we decided to apply to make a joint visit to Nuristan. It was a part of the country with mystery attached to it, because, though not far from Kabul, it was considered essentially out of bounds. It was said to be an extremely mountainous area without roads, in some places without trails, with crude houses perched on vertiginous cliffs; inhabited by an ancient people who were unpredictable and often hostile, and whose origins were obscure. They had only been converted to Islam as late as the 1890s, at the point of the sword. Few Afghan officials had visited the area, let alone foreigners. To our surprise, approval came back from the Afghan Foreign Ministry for access to central Nuristan. We wasted no time and were off – to the unknown!

During our time in Kabul we each travelled to other remote parts of Afghanistan, and subsequently, in later postings, to other corners of the globe, but the days in Nuristan, with its unique echoes of the past, left with each of us an indelible imprint.

The careers of the three friends followed different paths after leaving Kabul but we kept in desultory contact over the years. After we had all retired, Kendrick came to Cambridge University in 2000/2001 on a visiting fellowship arranged with the help of Barrington, who had a home in the city. Schlagintweit, who lived not far away in Bonn, had recently visited Cambridge and also seen Barrington there briefly. We discovered we had each kept some material relating to the Nuristan trip, despite deterioration due to the lapse of time. At Kendrick's initiative, the three of us decided that it was worth pooling our memories, records and photographs of the old journey to Nuristan, and putting them in the public domain.

It was as these pages were slowly being drawn together that the terrorist attacks of 11 September took place against New York City, and other targets. Within weeks the United States and its allies began operations against Osama bin Laden and his Al-Qaeda associates, who had been responsible for the attacks, and the Taliban administration in Afghanistan, which had given them a safe haven.

As had happened in the past (and as bin Laden must have realised would happen), it was the Afghan people who were the ones to suffer. Already victims of a Communist coup and the Soviet invasion, the anarchy of Mujahideen warlords and the Taliban's cruel mismanagement, they had also been subject to a long and debilitating drought. For over 20 years of 'Kalashnikov culture' most children had had no proper education. Thousands were refugees. Now the land was again in the throes of war.

All aspects of Afghanistan suddenly became of interest once again to the international community, and the job of producing this book seemed even more worthwhile. Nuristan was on the sidelines but was bound to be affected by the changes that would flow from a new and more democratic government, if this could be achieved. It is hoped that the special way of life of the Nuristanis can be largely preserved. These thoughts are expressed in what follows.

Introduction

Nuristan is a mountainous region in eastern Afghanistan, situated on the southern slopes of the high Hindu Kush range, where a number of rivers flow, often in narrow gorges, to join the Kabul and Kunar rivers, and eventually the Indus. The region is bordered on the east by the frontier with Chitral, in Pakistan, and on the west by the Panjshir Valley, famous recently as the home of Ahmad Shah Masud, and the centre of determined resistance to the Soviets and the Taliban. In the south the area flattens out into fertile plains and the hinterland of the town of Jalalabad (see map B).

The Nuristanis are concentrated in six main valleys and divided broadly into three groups: the white-clothed (Sefid Posh), black-clothed (Siah Posh) and the Parun people in the centre. Their languages are differentiated and unique. Their neighbours to the west are the Panjshiri Tajiks (basically Persian or 'Dari' speakers) and to the north, over the passes, the mountain Tajiks of Munjan. To the east lies Chitral, now part of Pakistan but once an independent state, which, for a time, exacted tribute from eastern Nuristan. It includes three small valleys of people called the Kalash, related to the Nuristanis, although speaking a different Dardic language. Almost half of the Kalash still follow the old polytheistic religion. Farthest south-east, along the Kunar river and in the lower Pech Valley, are the Pushtu-speaking Safis. There are other Pushtuns in the Laghman Valley to the south of Nuristan and around Jalalabad, but between these and the Nuristanis live a people, the Pashai, who have certain characteristics in common with the Nuristanis but a language with more Indian words. Gujers, nomadic herders speaking lowland Indian dialects, can also be found infiltrating parts of eastern Nuristan (see map C).

Although there were many legends about Kafiristan, and some Kafir traders and prisoners had been seen outside their territory, no visitors

1

had penetrated into the area itself until the end of the nineteenth century. Kipling chose Kafiristan as the mysterious land where a couple of British adventurers found themselves elected leaders, in his famous short story 'The Man Who Would be King', written in 1888. It was later made into a film with Sean Connery.

It was soon after this, in the early 1890s, that George Robertson (subsequently Sir George) took the initiative to visit eastern Nuristan. He was a British doctor and civil servant, Agent in Gilgit, who obtained permission to travel alone from Chitral to explore Kafiristan. He stayed for almost a year, mainly in Kamdesh, on the Bashgul river, which has been considered the leading Nuristani town, probably because it has been the most accessible. He also crossed over to the north of the Parun Valley. His book *The Kafirs of the Hindukush* was published in 1896.

Like many British officials of that era, he was an assiduous scholar as well as a brave explorer. In his book and other writings he set out in painstaking detail the information he had gleaned from the eastern Siah Posh and Parun Kafirs among whom he had lived. He described their character and physical attributes, their clothing, houses, sports and pastimes (including music and dance), their religious ceremonies and their predilection for fighting. He explained their reasonably democratic system of government, with elected leaders, and their customs. These included the important tradition that prominent individuals were expected to provide feasts for the people. A copy of Robertson's *Kafirs of the Hindukush* can still be found in Kipling's library at Batemans, his home in Sussex.

The society that Robertson described, in many ways a happy and self-contained one, was radically altered a few years later when the area was incorporated by force into the Afghan state, and – in theory at least – converted to Islam. There were no other outside visitors, or records of the area, for many years.

A German team had visited parts of Nuristan in the 1930s, apparently to look for 'Aryans', but no records existed, or were available. Western Nuristan was visited by Eric Newby in the 1950s, whose entertaining travel book, *A Short Walk in the Hindukush*, caught the imagination of a wide public. He and his companion, the British diplomat Hugh

Carless, encountered Wilfred Thesiger, one of the last great explorers, in the Ramgul Valley. The only foreigners who seem to have spent much time in the central Pech-Parun and Waigel Valleys were members of the Third Danish Central Asian Expedition, who were there in 1948/1949 and 1953/1954. (They made later visits in 1964 and 1970.) Records of their early trips were not available to us. Their most prominent member, Lennart Edelberg, subsequently published a number of works, with fine photographs.

Few educated Afghans had penetrated the Nuristani valleys except for occasional hunting trips. King Zaher Shah had visited Waigel in 1955, and the Amir Habibullah (see 'History' annex) was assassinated in the Alingar Valley in 1919.

* * *

The core of this book is Barrington's day-by-day narrative of our visit, written shortly after the event, covering some of the colourful characters that we encountered, together with those contemporary photographs that the three of us managed to preserve. Schlagintweit was the best photographer, and some of his black and white pictures seemed particularly fine. Despite having access to the famous British Embassy Residence Library there were no maps to be found of any sort of accuracy or usefulness. Barrington drew up a working map, which he hoped would prove to be reasonably reliable. It indicates the route we took (see map D).

Complementary to the narrative is Kendrick's more detailed, one might say anthropological, report, also written soon after our return, covering the tribal structure, houses, dress, diet, economy, etc. of the Sefid Posh Nuristanis. Some of the habits and customs of the people have now disappeared. Although this book is not intended as a scientific or academic treatise the material will contribute to studies of the Nuristani people, who had developed their own way of life, virtually isolated for thousands of years. We visited three of the main tribes, if one can call them tribes: one of the academic authorities on the region, Professor Jettmar, has suggested that the Nuristanis are organised into 'confederations of villages' rather than tribes. The fine picture book

Nuristan, jointly written by Edelberg and an American anthropologist working in Oxford, Schuyler Jones, included fuller anthropological information when it was published in 1979. Conditions have changed, however, even since those accounts were written. For example, some of the villages, including Wama, have been moved down from their crags closer to the river, as mentioned in Schlagintweit's 'Reflections', below. Access to water and convenience for transport has presumably become more important than defence.

The intriguing old religion of the Kafirs is touched on several times in our reports. A comprehensive account, mentioning all known Gods and many of the ceremonies, is to be found in Jettmar's *Religions of the Hindu Kush*. Volume I of his work covers Nuristan, the only volume that has so far been translated into English. One interesting point he brings out is that the peaceful Parun Valley seems to have been the religious sanctuary of all the Kafirs.

* * *

Since our story was 40 years old, it was decided to include reflections by the three co-authors of this book, by now experienced and worldly-wise. There is some overlap, but each of us looks back with a different perspective. In particular, Kendrick concentrates more on recent tragic events and what he considers to be some of the elements of US foreign policy that have contributed to them. We would all agree that foreign ministries in the Western democracies cannot afford to ignore smaller countries, however remote, in the modern, interdependent world. Barrington's last post was not far away, in Pakistan. In retirement after 11 September he found himself in demand to give talks on the history of Afghanistan, and he has even played the role of pundit on a TV programme on the subject. Schlagintweit, active as head of UNICEF in Germany, has remained involved in political and economic developments in the area.

The annexes include Barrington's summary history of Afghanistan from early times to the present day, as background to the study of Nuristan and current events. Also some opinions, and information, about the origin of the Nuristani people, which will remain contentious until resolved – perhaps – by DNA evidence. There follows a selective bibliography of relevant books, almost all in English, several of which are referred to in the body of this publication. Some of the latest books on Afghanistan are included, even if they contain few references to Nuristan. Unfortunately, many of the older books are out of print, and can be found only in libraries or, if you are lucky, in second-hand bookshops. We conclude with biographical material showing the authors' varied careers, as a sort of personal epilogue. Sadly, J.T. Kendrick, to whose memory this book is dedicated, died in January 2003.

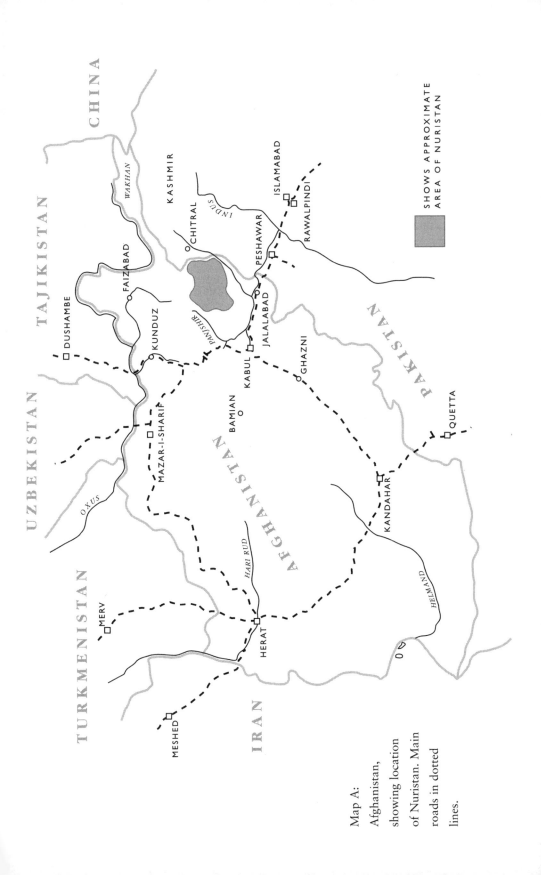

Map A:
Afghanistan,
showing location
of Nuristan. Main
roads in dotted
lines.

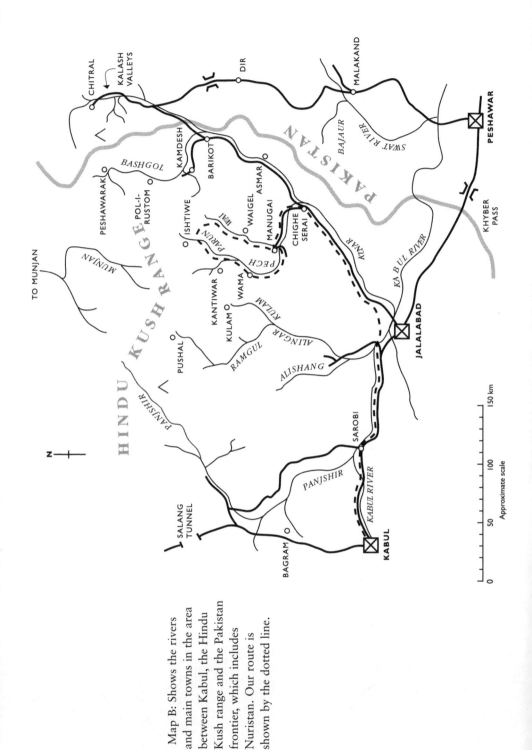

Map B: Shows the rivers and main towns in the area between Kabul, the Hindu Kush range and the Pakistan frontier, which includes Nuristan. Our route is shown by the dotted line.

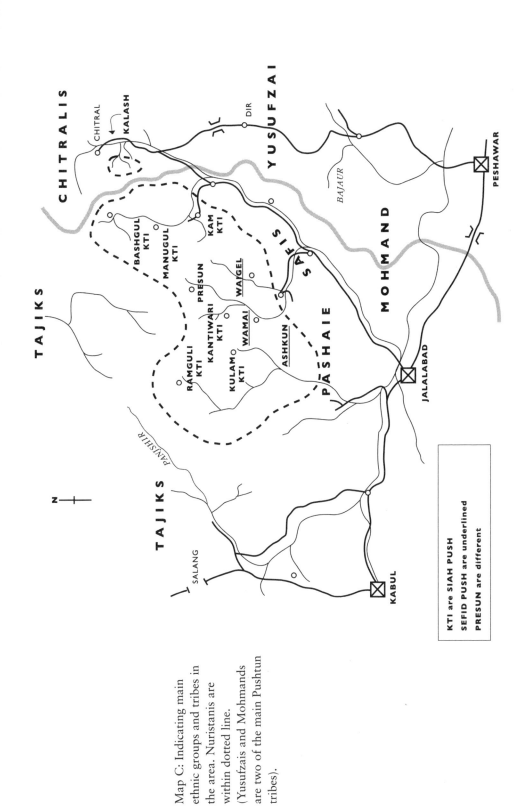

Map C: Indicating main
ethnic groups and tribes in
the area. Nuristanis are
within dotted line.
(Yusufzais and Mohmands
are two of the main Pushtun
tribes).

KTI are SIAH PUSH
SEFID PUSH are underlined
PRESUN are different

CHITRALIS

KALASH

CHITRAL

DIR

YUSUFZAI

BAJAUR

PESHAWAR

TAJIKS

BASHGUL
KTI

MANUGUL
KTI

KAM
KTI

PRESUN

WAGEL

SAFIS

KANTIWARI
KTI

WAMAI

RAMGULI
KTI

KULAM
KTI

ASHKUN

PASHAIE

MOHMAND

PANISHIR

JALALABAD

TAJIKS

SALANG

KABUL

N

OUR ROUTE

Map D (facing page): This map, a part of Nuristan in contrast to the others, dates from 1960, when no accurate maps of the area were available. This was the best representation that Barrington could make of our route on foot in the two main river valleys, slightly adjusted after our return. See introduction to the narrative. It was our working map.

Our route is marked by the dotted line, continuous when travelled by vehicles, dotted when by foot. The broad areas of the different Nuristani tribes are indicated, as is what we were told about the various mountain passes.

The rivers are mostly in deep gorges and twist more than indicated. The villages not marked as being on one of the two main rivers were mostly way up in the mountains.

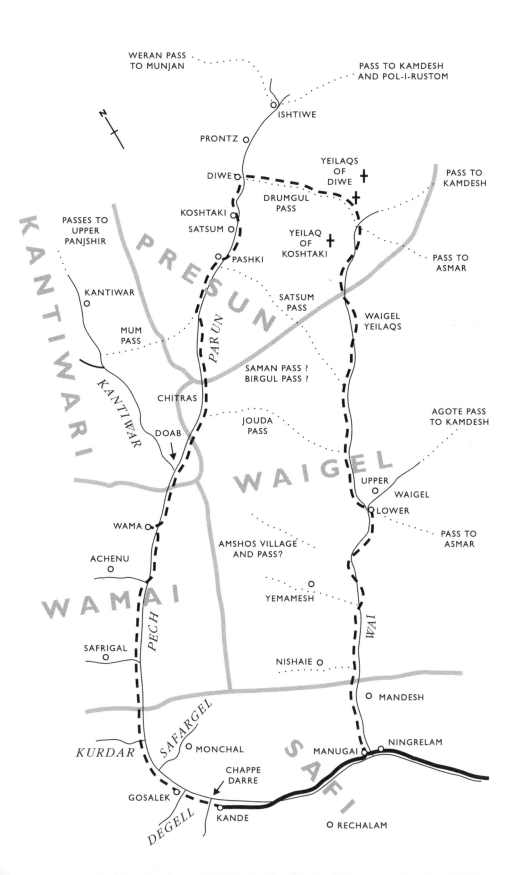

1 Account of a Journey to Two Valleys in Nuristan (Kafiristan) in July 1960

Nicholas Barrington

British Embassy, Kabul

1960

The idea of travelling to Nuristan was originally that of Mr J.T. Kendrick ('JT'), second secretary at the United States embassy, who invited first me, and then Reinhard Schlagintweit of the German embassy, to join him on a trip to the Pech (commonly known in this spelling, although pronounced 'Pich') Valley in central Nuristan.

Kendrick had first tried to get permission to go to the Bashgul Valley and the country around Kamdesh in eastern Nuristan. Kamdesh is the largest and most famous of the Nuristan villages, the scene of the activities of Sir George Robertson, the only man who has recorded for posterity the way of life of the Kafirs before Abdur Rahman's conversion of them in the 1890s, and I think the only place in Nuristan ruled directly by a representative of the Afghan government (it is the centre of a Hokumat-e Mahal – basic administrative unit). But, whether because of the new road that is being built up that particular valley to Badakhsan or for some other reason, Kamdesh is still strictly out of bounds to all diplomats from Kabul, and permission was refused.

The Pech Valley, as opposed to Kamdesh, is not within the forbidden frontier zone, and so we merely informed the Ministry of Foreign Affairs that we were going there, though JT did, I am told, get an oral assurance that there would be no objection. What we did not know until we arrived at the mouth of the valley, however, was that an officer and two men of the Kabul police had been told to accompany us all the way

13

for 'protection'. We got to know our police escort pretty well by the end of the trip, but we never really found out why they were there. Was it because the authorities expected trouble with the locals, because they suspected that we might engage in subversive activities, or because they thought that, when officers from three different embassies went out together, things ought to be made as smooth for them as possible? We shall never know.

One essential prerequisite was the approval and favour of the governor of Jalalabad and the Eastern Province, H. E. Ghulam Faruq Osman. This dynamic little old individual, called 'Wazir Sahib' in his province (suggesting minister rank), is related to, and influential with, the court of Kabul, and has undoubtedly a very free hand in his own province. He has the reputation of being honest, tough and very much on the ball, and he is feared and obeyed by his subordinates, because they know that if he says they are to go – they go. Afghan friends in Kabul again and again reminded us to call on the governor and get his personal OK before we started on our journey. In fact, Osman was well informed of our plans, and made all the arrangements that he could for us. Perhaps it was a good thing that we contacted his son Toryalai (who works in the Ministry of Foreign Affairs) beforehand, because he certainly told his father all about us; also, we telephoned the governor himself two days before our departure asking if we could see him in Jalalabad on the way up to the Kunar Valley. In the event, he told us that he would be up the valley himself, and would meet us in Chighe Serai. When we got to that place, he was farther north still with the Hakem-e Kelan (regime administrator) of Chighe Serai in Kamdesh, but we had reason to be very grateful for the way he had arranged everything for us, and we sent him a warm letter of appreciation when the trip was over. It became apparent that his goodwill was essential to the success of any trip in the area. (Osman was removed from office shortly after these events, because, it was said, of the Bajaur episode. This was an incursion by armed tribesmen into Bajaur, inside Pakistan, which created an international incident. Osman may have been made a scapegoat.)

Since we had only ten days at our disposal, we decided that the best use of the time would be to drive as far as we could up the Pech Valley, then walk up the valley as far as we could, come back and find a pass to cross over into the Waigel Valley, and finally come down to the bottom of that valley to meet up again with the cars. Our actual route will be seen from map D. There were no maps of the area with any accuracy that I could discover and this was the best I could do. The map was adjusted somewhat after our return to take account of topography that we experienced, including how long it took to walk between villages. Both rivers, particularly the Waigel, wind and twist more than shown. We did not, unfortunately, get right to the end of the Parun Valley; on the other hand, we were able to cross straight over into the Waigel Valley without retracing our steps, and so ended up much further in that valley than we expected to. By choosing this route, we passed through the areas of three quite different Nuristani tribes: the Wamai, the Presun and the Waigel.

TUESDAY, 5 JULY 1960

We started early; at 5:00 a.m. I was in my own Land-Rover, with an embassy driver (Reza Khan), and in Reinhard's Land-Rover were Reinhard himself, JT and our translator, Kheir Mohammad. The latter was an intelligent, cheerful fellow, with a somewhat negroid face, slightly running to fat. He was working as a counterpart in the US Aid agency, having finished technical school, and claimed to have travelled into Nuristan when he was a student in Jalalabad. We soon found that he had never got very far! He came from Jalalabad, and spoke Pashtu, which none of us did.

With us in the cars we carried the minimum of personal clothing, and about 40 tins of food (about one per person per day), as well as sleeping bags, inflatable mattresses, medicines and presents to give away. We had one hurricane lamp and one stove between us.

We stopped for a second breakfast with a young Austrian who lives by the dam at Sarobi, where he works. He showed us the newspaper articles written by Herman Philipovich, who travelled up 'our' valley a year before. We were disappointed by the articles, which were sensational, and contained little useful information.

Lower Kunar river. Preparing a raft by inflating animal skins.

At the Darrunta Bridge we threw the name of the governor around (he was then up the way we were going), and got permission to cross. After crossing the Kabul river, the road runs back along its north bank to the west, and then turns off (unmarked) into the desert. For some hours we drove north over the flat, arid, stony desert – and most of the stones seemed to be on the road – until we came at last to the green and cultivated area that is called Shewa. Just afterwards, looking up to the left, you can see the entrance to the beautiful Darre Nur. It was about this time that I had to stop with some petrol pump trouble, and was overtaken by a jeep full of police wearing Kabul uniforms. A young officer asked if he could help, then told me that they had come out especially to protect and look after us. When we went on, they kept well behind, and did not bother us. North of Shewa the country was very beautiful, with the road running by the side of the vast, fast-flowing Kunar river.

At one place we stopped opposite a ruined castle in a place called Narang, and talked to some Pathans who were standing by. These were Safis, and they told us the story of the castle, which had belonged to a local Khan called Mir Zaman, who had taken part in the Safi rebellion, and had ultimately, like many of his tribe, lost his head and his lands. Little is known about the great Safi rebellion of 1949 in Kabul, but the memory of that time must be fresh in the Safi country, for everywhere we saw ruined forts, and heard stories of the fate of the great Safi leaders. Shahsowar and Salim Khan were the main leaders of that revolt, but everywhere the Khans supported them, and their tribal armies nearly took the fort at Jalalabad. Eventually they were crushed by troops from Kabul, and the leaders were killed. The King, we were told, wept to hear that they had been killed, but he still banished all their sons and close relatives to distant parts of Afghanistan, and his government took over their lands. Some of these exiled Safis have been doing very well in more fertile parts of the country, and do not wish to return. On the way back, in the same Kunar Valley, we met a group of Safis who had been visiting their exiled relatives in Kunduz. They were most impressed by the prosperity there, and thought their relatives very lucky.

After a pleasant picnic lunch under some trees on a little grassy promontory by the river, and a swim, we drove on to Chighe Serai, where we arrived at about 3:30 p.m., earlier than we had expected. We stopped at the small group of government buildings, and had tea in the 'scenic lounge', which looked out to the north over the Pech river, to the valley we wanted to enter. In the courtyard were crowds of venerable Safi maleks summoned to meet the governor, in front of whom they would compose their troubles, but the governor was not there – he had gone on with the Hakem-e Kelan of Chighe Serai to Kamdesh. The governor had, however, made arrangements for us, because soon after we arrived a short, middle-aged and rather scruffy man appeared and introduced himself as the Hakem (local administrator) of Darre Pech, Mohammad Ibrahim Khan. Although a bit bothered by our police escort, he was very friendly and helpful, and did not try to stop us making plans to go right up into

A group crossing the lower Kunar river.

Nuristan. He would accompany us all the way, he said. Perhaps he had
been softened up by the governor. He wanted us to come straightaway
with him and spend the night in his Hokumati (local headquarters), and
this suited us very well.

Also at the hotel was a striking person dressed in white, with a white
cap, and a vivid red and green shawl thrown over his shoulder. He was the
first Nuristani that we saw, and, though we realised later that his clothes
had been quite untypical, he looked magnificent. He was from Waigel, and
had a fine face with strong yet sensitive features. He had great dignity, and
was quick and intelligent. I told him where we wanted to go, and
mentioned the towns – Wama, Pashki, Ishtiwe and Waigel – that I had
read about. Though they were in his area, the Hakem seemed to have

heard of none of them, but the Nuristani, who must have been some
sort of government clerk, confirmed that these places were real and not
imaginary, and that the itinerary I proposed was possible. We were much
relieved, because we had had no idea of the distances involved. We made
tentative approaches to the Nuristani to see whether he would come
with us as a guide, but he was disturbed by our police escort, and said
he would meet us in his village, Waigel. He never did.

We bought rice and matches in Chighe Serai, and, though there was
no petrol to be had, established that we had enough to get us to Darre
Pech and back. Then we left with the Hakem and his personal armed
soldier for the delightful two-hour drive to his Hokumati, at a little
village in the Darre Pech called Manugai. We drove up and down by the
north bank of the river, which was in spate. Clean and sparkling, it was
wider than the Kabul river below Sarobi. The hills were dry, but the
valley itself was green and beautiful. Down by the river were masses of
large, pink and white, waxy oleanders. In one little village a woman
with her breasts half exposed who was arguing violently with a man,
surrounded by a crowd of villagers, tried to stop our car, but we horned
our way past. The Safis are famous for woman trouble – they sleep with
each other's wives, and shoot each other for doing so. We were told later
that there were many deaths every year from this cause. 'A wild and
crazy lot,' said one soldier from distant Herat, who was doing his national
service with the Hakem's troops.

Eventually we crossed a bridge over the Waigel river, then turned back
up the hill to the village of Manugai, our journey's base and starting point.
Having shaken hands with every member of the reception committee, we
left our cars at the end of the road at the south end of the village, and, with
porters carrying our things, walked round to the north and higher side to
the Hakem's official residence, where we and everything else were dumped
on the roof. Here beds were laid out for us, and tea was produced. The
view was magnificent, looking down past the villages of Manugai on the
right, and Ningrelam on the left, to the Pech Valley, in the soft evening
light. Way down to our left, the Wai river rushed noisily down our little
valley to join the other.

After a cup of tea we went down to wash by the river, but found this
difficult, due to the irritatingly close presence of the policemen. It turned

The valley of Ningrelam.

out that they were genuinely worried that we would try to bathe in
the hurtling water and get swept away – which would certainly have
been unpleasant for them. We returned to a splendid pilau supper,
with most refreshing mint 'dugh' (yoghurt and water). It turned out that
our friend the Hakem, who was terribly proud of his symbol of
authority, an antiquated telephone, which was with him on a little table
on the roof, was a Pashtun from Wardak, who had been a Hakem for 15
years in different places all over the Eastern Province.

    After supper we asked the police officer, Lieutenant Abdul Azim, to
come up and have tea with us. Then we tried to persuade him to stay
behind and send only one man with us on the trip, explaining that the
bigger our party was the more trouble we would create for the local

The Hakem of Manugai on the roof of his house. His phone is a symbol of authority.

people, and this was the last thing we wanted. When he said that the people would be nicer to us if police were around we begged to differ, saying that some of the police's unpopularity might be transferred to us. I wasn't quite sure enough of some nuances in what he said to know whether he wanted to be bribed or not. In the end, we saw each other's points of view, and decided in favour of a call to the governor – but the telephone would not work. Thus the police, who had obviously been told to stay with us, had no alternative but to do so. By the end of the trip we both admired and liked our police escort. The young officer, who was newly commissioned, was intelligent and friendly – and plucky too on the mountain. He gave himself no airs over his men. The two policemen who came with us were both, also, tough, friendly and intelligent. Specially picked, I should think, and probably shortly to be commissioned themselves. One, Abdul Ghafur, was the son of a wealthy merchant who was thinking of buying a Land-Rover. They came out with practically nothing except a blanket, thinking that we were going for a day's climb into the mountains, but they stuck with us all the way. They had no change of clothes, so that their uniform and boots were in shreds by the time we had finished. They never complained, and they never bothered us by impinging on our privacy, or stopping us talking to the local people. On our return it was difficult to commend them sufficiently to the authorities without making it seem that they had been too friendly.

It was cool up on the roof, but somehow I didn't get much sleep that night. Perhaps it was the excitement. Perhaps it was the brightness of the moonlight.

WEDNESDAY, 6 JULY

We rose late and did not have breakfast until 6:00 a.m., by which time the sun was up over the mountains and it was hot. Eventually, with much fussing and farewells, we got off. It turned out that the Hakem, who had told us in Chighe Serai that he would go with us everywhere we went, had no intention of leaving even his own little village. He sent with us instead his 'Kotowal Sahib', the head clerk of his police, one of the senior officials of his little organisation. He also sent two soldiers, one huge and one tiny. These out of his complement of 53. But none of them lasted very long. We persuaded them all to turn back and come to meet us seven days later in Waigel.

It took us about two hours to drive from Manugai to Kande, which was where the Aliqadari was, and the end of the road. (An Aliqadari is the lowest unit of administration, reporting to a Hokumat-e Mahal.) Another beautiful drive this, with an exciting road – sometimes very steep, sometimes very rutted, sometimes through the river, often high up at the side of the valley with a fine view. We came upon Kande before we expected it, a tiny mud village with one or two shady places under branches of huge chenar trees. In one of these, in the centre of the village,

Fields of lower Pech Valley – where the trek begins.

sat the friendly little Aliqadar, recently come from Kabul, waiting for us. His name was Abdur Rahim. He offered us tea, plums and most refreshing watermelons (brought all the way from Kabul). Then he helped us decide finally about the composition of our party. He insisted that we take with us two of his local soldiers (who were, we were glad to see, in civilian clothes) and his Sar Kateb-e Ehsaye (meaning in charge of recruitment), Mr Amir Mohammad, as a guide. All of these knew the Pech-Parun Valley well. The Sar Kateb, who was plump, with shifty eyes, and who wore a little red velvet skullcap, had been up the valley several times to recruit conscripts from the villages. He was well known wherever we went. He caused us a great deal of amusement because, although he professed to be tough, and tried to persuade us to go in short stages for our own sake, we gradually realised that he was the sufferer. He used to arrive well after us, panting heavily, and he was always thinking of his stomach and his bed!

We accepted the offer of the guide, but insisted that the Kotowal Sahib and his two soldiers return to the Hokumati, which they did without much reluctance. We also engaged six porters to carry all our things – food, tents, clothes, stoves, etc. – at a rate of Afs. 10 a day, plus food. Five of them were Safis and, of these five, three stayed with us to the end of our journey, for which we were very grateful. The Safis are an interesting tribe; although they speak Pashtu and call themselves Pashtuns, they are one of the fringe Pashtun tribes with a doubtful pedigree, and they seem to have more delicate features than the ordinary Pathan. Caroe mentions that they admit to being recent converts to Islam, and therefore are unusually fanatical (some of them live in the valleys of Bajaur – and the Akhund of Swat was a Safi). It is possible that they are a Pashtunised tribe of Nuristani-type origin.

One of the porters was a real live Nuristani, from Wama, our first goal. He had fine striking features, and was strongly built, and he was wearing real Nuristani clothes: a squashed Chitrali hat, a grey shirt, thick buff-coloured trousers that hung straight and stiff without creases to just below the knee, and black leggings wound tightly round his calves, making them look even more muscular than they were. The police engaged an extra porter to carry their belongings.

Before setting out we visited an elaborate camp on the other side of the village, under some more chenars. This was a base for the French geological team who were making a brief survey of the area. They had got no farther than Wama and the beginning of the Waigel Valley, and spent most of their time in the Chappe Darre, where beryllium is to be found and which joins the Pech at Kande itself. The French team was, as always, superbly organised for camping. After a glass of juice with them we set off up the road by the river at a brisk pace. Reza Khan, my Pakistani driver, stayed behind here to look after our two vehicles, and to get them back to our point of exit from the mountains, which was to be Manugai, where the Hokumati was. He told us afterwards that the Aliqadar, with whom he had stayed for three days, had been most kind to him and hospitable.

In an hour or so we reached the biggish village of Gosalek and crossed our first single-plank bridge over the Degell river, which debouches here into the Pech. Here 'Fatty', the Sar Kateb Sahib, wanted to stop for lunch, and even for the night, but we pushed on relentlessly, only stopping for a cup of dugh with the local maleks, of whom there were four. They were the leaders (and biggest landowners) in the village, and its representatives as far as the government was concerned. The honour was obviously inherited, since two of the four maleks were quite young. I had a longish talk with the chief mullah (chief of six mullahs) in the village, who was Kabul-educated, but who had retired from active government work as a Qazi (or judge), and merely judged local disputes when asked. He was rather impressive, with a deep red chupan (or cloak), and was obviously

The Pech River.

keeping the locals up to scratch by the way they bowed to him on the road. Apparently he had no prejudice about foreigners. He and two of the maleks accompanied us on the way to the boundaries of the village.

The path was lovely, up and down, always alongside the rushing, foaming river, over rocks by the water, through cultivated fields, up the steep mountainsides. Around us were much holly and other trees and mint and many other herbs. At times the path was difficult, and then we realised why since we had arrived in this part of the country there had never been any question of our going by horse, or using horses for our baggage. We were going somewhere where horses and donkeys could not go. We saw not one of these animals on our trip. There were goats and sheep and cows up in the valleys for food, but no beasts of burden. Everything had to be carried up to those remote areas on somebody's back.

By one o'clock we reached some shady trees by the river, the domain of a local (Safi) Khan, who had a big house there. The place was called Deranik. Besides the big house there were only a few cottages. The Khan and his retainers insisted on bringing us charpoys and magnificent quilts and blankets all the way from the house. We washed, ate the remains of the previous day's sandwich lunch, together with mast (yoghurt), mulberries and tea provided by the Khan, and then relaxed to the sound of the rushing water. After one and a half hours we tried to get moving, but found that our companions were determined to stay put. They were waiting for a pilau lunch that was being prepared in the big house. As we were determined to go on, however, one of the soldiers, a young Pashtun called Astane Gol, was sent with us (plus a stick, which was our only protection until he cut one for me too from the undergrowth). We were happy to be alone and uncluttered on the edge of Nuristan – a Nuristan that still seemed very elusive and distant. Our soldier helped us to wade across the Kurdar river coming in from our left, and told us that this was a hard but possible way over to the Alingar Valley and Laghman. According to reports, Pashaie people live in Kurdar. As the afternoon wore on, the path became steeper, and the hills closed in. The valley we were in was now running roughly north and south, its sides were dark green with holly and other bushes, and at its bottom lay the silver ribbon of the river. Far away in the distance, the V of the valley ended in a great mountain of rock bathed in the evening sunlight. Astane Gol pointed with his stick. 'That's it!' 'What?' 'That's Wama!' How exciting the magical name was for us, as full of associations as Xanadu, and still just as remote!

On we walked into the evening. I found that some chewing gum I had brought was a success; it kept the saliva going, and stopped the dryness in the mouth. Eventually we reached the mouth of the Safrigal Valley. Here Astane Gol told us that the way we had to go was to the left, up to the village; those had been Fatty's instructions, and he also told us that it would take at least an hour or two to climb up to

In the heart of the Pech Valley – the dark spot on the edge of the promontory is the village of Wama.

the village – which was, we gathered, like so many others around, perched on a rock. We had a long conference. Reinhard and I did not like being dictated to, and did not want to be deflected from our course. JT was neutral, but inclined to agree with the guide. But three is a good number – there is always a majority some way – and we decided, to the distress of our soldier, to go on for an hour or so and then camp. The porters would have to follow. We left word with an old woman working in some small fields by the junction. Then we went on over a path that became increasingly difficult, and after an hour came to a perfect camping spot – a flat green place under the steep hill down close to the river. It was well shaded by trees that looked like fig trees, with heart-shaped leaves. We put down our loads (mainly cameras; we soon gave up all ideas of trying to carry knapsacks – it was too much like unnecessary hard work!), and had not rested more than ten minutes before, like something out of Stanley and Livingstone, a party of men came out of the trees in front of us. It was the leader of the French geological expedition, with Seyyed Hashem, his counterpart from the Ministry of Mines, and their train of porters and guides. They were as astonished to see us as we were to see them, and sat down for 20 minutes and joined us for a chat. They had been to Wama, but not up to the village, and gave us some accurate information about that place and showed us their maps (just rivers – copied from aerial photographs, but very useful). We gave them the news from Kabul.

After they had gone we waited a bit and then began to collect sticks for a fire. I found a good stout stick, which I used as a walking stick for a little while. It began to get dark, and we wondered where our baggage had got to, when all of a sudden the translator, the police and our porters came crashing through the bushes behind us on to our campsite. Fatty was a bit annoyed because he had to send two porters back in the dark to collect food from Safrigal. We had supper – soup, sausages, bread and tea – and then unrolled our sleeping bags, blew up our mattresses and went to bed. I had chosen a flat place under an overhanging rock, but was a bit uncertain about it, and was relieved when a porter told me not to put my bed there because there might be snakes in such a place! It was chilly, and the porters and others were sitting round two huge fires waiting patiently for their food. We gave them some tea and a pot to boil it in and went to sleep. At one o'clock I woke up to see their yellow faces round the fire, and someone holding aloft a great fowl that they had just slaughtered and were going to roast. They had bought four of them. The sound of the water so close was deafening.

THURSDAY, 7 JULY

I was woken at 5:15 a.m. by the sound of Reinhard breaking sticks. We were up and eating and ready to be off as soon as possible, but still found the porters, who like to start early in the cool, waiting impatiently for us. Two of the porters were paid off and exchanged for new ones, presumably from Safrigal (I am not sure whether this village is Nuristani or Safi, but I think it is the last Safi village). Soon after we started we had to cross a very nasty bit of slippery rock just above the torrent. I went on with the Nuristani porter, whose name was 'Kah' (emphatic)! Reinhard was ahead and we eventually caught up with him; JT was behind with the main body. The Nuristani was tough and fast and, eventually, although he was carrying a heavy knapsack, could not stand our slow pace and went ahead. A lot of the way he ran. He taught us that 'agus maestus' was the Nuristani (Wamai) for 'manda nabashi', the Persian greeting to someone passed on the road, meaning 'may you not be tired'! If he had not been with us at the beginning we might never have attempted to get across one very nasty part, where the river had run right across the path up against a vertical rock. We had to take off our shoes and balance on piles of stones under the water, which was swirling about our legs. It was icy!

Then on the road we met one or two people who were obviously Nuristanis – we had arrived at last! The two of us were alone, in the fabulous land of Nuristan. At the junction of the Achenu Valley with the Pech, the path crossed over to the eastern side of the river, doing so by means of a fantastically engineered single-plank bridge. Below the bridge the water was cascading furiously into a minor version of the Niagara Falls. I was first over, and took a picture of Reinhard crossing;

The Pech in July, when the snow melts in the Hindu Kush.

then he suggested that I should go back so that he could take me. I found it very difficult indeed to turn round in the middle of the bridge! After this we rested and drank deep from the cold river water. We always drank river water, and never had any ill effects. In a glass it looked amazingly clean, and probably was so, because of the fast flow. According to reports, the people of Achenu are Ashkuns.

It was shadier on the other bank of the river, and the path often wove through lush grass down by the river, but we got very tired, and, when we saw a perfect pool with a pebbly bottom formed by a fast-flowing little stream tinkling off a high rock like a shower, we undressed and had a perfect swim. We found we could rinse our grimy hair under the shower. We dried ourselves in the sun, ate mulberries off a tree and

Nicholas on single-plank bridge across the Pech, where the track crossed the river.

swam again. After a time an old white-bearded porter, who was always ahead of the others, passed us, but he was so shocked by our nudity that he kept his head down and would not even tell us how far behind the others were! Then, refreshed, we dressed and went on until, rounding a corner, we found ourselves face to face over the river with the great mountain of rock that we had seen from afar the day before. Way up above us, perched halfway up the rock, was a dark patch that we soon made out to be the roofs of tiny distant houses. This was Wama. We soon came to another precarious bridge, the bridge of Wama itself, and lay down to rest on a wooden platform under the shade of some walnut trees on the other side. We were directly under, though 1000 or more feet under, the village of Wama, but we had no intention of attempting

Woman on balcony overlooking Wama in the early morning.

the climb until we had eaten and rested. When JT and the porters arrived about an hour later we ate raisins and melted chocolate cooled in water, and drank salt water to counteract perspiration. We had soup and accepted some local buttermilk, which did grave damage to our insides. Then we dozed long until 4:30 p.m., when we organised our things and started the stiff climb up the hill. It was very tiring – just like walking up a very bad and uneven flight of stairs for half an hour. As we went up into the sky the river and the bridge became tiny below us. One or two scenic platforms had been built as resting places, and on some little ledges single stone graves were huddled. Eventually we saw the log roofs of the first houses, and groups of children watching us from them. I had had a feeling of being watched for some time.

We went up between the houses along a sort of narrow street, watched silently from all sides, until we came to a sort of square. There we were met by a tall, distinguished man in a great brown cloth cloak, a young man of obvious importance, and a group of senior villagers, who were our reception committee. The houses around us were clinging to the steep rock. They were made of horizontal logs of wood, resting on top of each other at the corners, the spaces being filled in with mud and stones. The flat roof of one house was the yard and road in front of the one above. We were taken to a big spare roof kept for guests, because it had no house above it – only a steep wall of rock. On this incomparable site four beds were brought for the translator and us and covered with rugs. Facing us, the ground dropped

Wama rooftops, overlooking the Pech river – 1000 feet to the valley floor.

Wama houses clutching the cliffs high above the Pech river.

away practically sheer to the bridge over 1000 feet below. To the right was an old tree that looked like a chestnut, beyond it a smaller roof where the police slept, and behind that a wall of rock. To our left rear a semicircle of wooden houses rose up back against the hill. There was a full moon coming up, the air was balmy, and the situation dramatic in the extreme.

The Wamais themselves made it more dramatic. With their leggings, trousers, jerkins and cloaks in neutral wool colours (a symphony of browns), with their brass-studded leather belts with daggers in them, with the occasional brilliantly coloured woven cloak, perhaps red, thrown over their shoulders in faultless folds, they looked like a cast from Macbeth who had strayed from Stratford. We were a little worried

Wama balcony and enclosed room.

about two of our loads that had not come up from the bottom of the hill, and after a time we got very worried about them. Then, suddenly, little Astane Gol appeared, covered with perspiration and carrying the double load. He had been left to guard them, and the porters had deserted him, so he brought them both up himself. He grinned when we praised him, and was given priority with the sweet tea.

The good-looking young man who first met us started giving orders for our comfort, and it became apparent that he was our host, the malek in fact, of this part of the village. Wama is divided into three parts, each with its own malek, mosque and mullah. We were in the lowest section, which had its own water from a spring. The others were round the hill and higher up. They had no water of their own, and had to carry it up from the river.

There were perhaps 300 houses in the whole village, 100 in the part we were in.

Our malek was 20 years old (about) and had two wives, one son and one daughter. His father had died when he was 11 years old, but he was not the eldest brother. The village chose him as the fittest to succeed as malek. He owned 20 cows and had people to work for him. A relation of his came and talked to us. He was the most magnificent-looking man there, about 45 years old, tall, with a fine black beard, and an intelligent and powerful face. He had a natural sense of how to carry his cloak. He seemed to be a former malek of one of the other parts of the village, but this was never quite clear. He spoke Persian well, and was fairly well informed. The two maleks, rather embarrassed,

Wama child sleeping under blanket over 1000 feet above Pech river.

sat and joined us for a chicken pilau when we had dinner, and tried to answer our many questions. They did not know when Wama had been founded. There is a strong tradition that the forefathers of these people lived lower down the Kunar Valley, and were chased up into the mountains, where they built this fortress so very high on its rock for defence. (The government has been offering them all sorts of inducements to try to get them to come down and live by the river, but in vain so far – fortunately for romanticists! These people are unhappy about their life, but will not change it.) The malek said that this happened quite recently, and associated it with Abdur Rahman's conquest of Nuristan, and yet the older malek quoted five or six generations of his fathers as having lived in Wama. It seems to me that the village must be more than 70 years old.

The old malek admitted that all the work was done by women, both in the house and in the fields. The only thing the men do besides sitting around and talking, is to look after the animals. Some of them go out every morning to the high pastures on top of the mountains to look after their flocks, and at lunchtime they eat the mast, milk and curds that is not available at home. We saw women working in the fields and collecting great bundles of firewood, but we did not see them in the village, just sometimes a flash of black as they went by.

The Wamais, we were told, sometimes intermarry with Waigelis, Kantiwaris and even Safis, but not with the Presuns, who are considered quite different (and inferior). Their relations with the other tribes are good, though they admitted that they fought for the government against the Safis during the Safi rebellion.

One of the highlights of my time in Wama was the visit to the bath and cloaks. On request I was conducted to the lavatory by a man with a burning brand. It consisted of a little log hut, and when I went in I saw that the floor was simply a series of wooden poles with nothing below them. The hut was built at the top of a cliff, and the excrement fell most hygienically 200 or 300 feet down into a gully. The bath was a round room entered by a low door. Halfway up the wall on the mountainside was a spout, along which a stream of fresh water came from a spring inside the rock, and fell in a neat curve into a well, from where it drained away to the rest of the village. It made an ideal shower, and there was a smooth piece of wood especially to stand on.

Gradually the three of us established our fields of operation. JT was treasurer and doctor, Reinhard was camping expert, and I, as the only Persian speaker, was translator and map-reader. Thus, when the young malek asked us to come and look at his sick brother, it was JT and I who went with him. On the way up to the hut, he pointed out a place where a rock had fallen from the mountain some years before and killed 12 people. Up in the hut we saw a bearded man turning feverishly on a small bed. The hut consisted of a single room that was used for everything – cooking, washing, sitting and sleeping – with four wooden pillars supporting the roof. It was dark, and the atmosphere was very oppressive. Eventually JT prescribed penicillin, and we gave the family most careful instructions on how to administer it. But it was impossible to diagnose what was wrong.

Sitting round the fire afterwards, we spoke of the old gods of Nuristan. They had heard of the two most famous: Imra, Jove in their pantheon, and Gish, the god of war; but they spoke reluctantly of them, I think because of the power and fanaticism of the local mullah, whom we heard calling the muezzin earlier in the evening. The mullah did not come to see us and would not even receive us, though we asked to pay our respects. I think it was the mullah also who scotched our desire to hear some local music. The maleks brought only one dirge-playing musician, who strummed a simple four-stringed harp. We did not think much of him, ordered him away, and went to bed under the stars.

FRIDAY, 8 JULY

Our hosts were tall and a bit grim, but we did not notice how forbidding they were till they began to argue with our translator about the price of the food and the new Nuristani porters whom we had to engage. Of course, without porters one is quite helpless, as some other travellers to Nuristan have discovered (see Thesiger). We were lucky to have the basic core of faithful Safis and, perhaps, to have the police

Wama – porters buying food.

with us as a show of force. We were woken irritatingly early, and had a poor breakfast (later we had to fill up with Ryvita and cheese; it is impossible to walk energetically on an empty stomach), and then left the translator, Kheir Mohammad, and the police to sort out the problem of porters etc., while we went on a tour of the village prior to setting out for the Parun Valley. It was only afterwards that we found out just how unpleasant things had been. Kheir Mohammad had been forced to promise Afs. 20 a day to the Wamai porters, and the maleks had refused to provide a porter for the police. The officer got angry and fired his pistol over their heads, and this made them furious. All of our party said they were delighted to be away from such unpleasant people. The situation must have been quite menacing with

Old men of Wama.

these rough men up on their own crags, in their brown robes, showing their claws.

We said goodbye and thanked the maleks and gave them presents, while JT dished out literature about Eisenhower (!). Then we went off for a good tour of the upper parts of the village, where the streets were either the roofs themselves or dusty channels running steeply between the houses. On one roof we stopped and talked to an old man with a long white beard called Ghulam Mohammad, who was full of life and intelligence. He said that he had been about seven years old at the time of Abdur Rahman's conquest of Nuristan, and he remembered the latter's general Ghulam Haider coming up the valley we had just come up. (We were looking back down it now and to the mountain beyond – a

Wama – Nicholas talking to the old man who had travelled to India.

staggering, top-of-the-world panorama.) He seemed rather proud of the fact that his father was a real Kafir, and that he was born one. He knew all about Imra and Gish but not Moni (Imra's deputy according to some). The temples, he said, had all been cut down. It seems that after the conquest he was attached to the King's court and had served the Amir Habibullah as a Shikari or attendant, or possibly as a soldier. He had served from the time of Abdur Rahman to the time of Nadir Shah. He happened to be one of the people chosen to accompany the Amir Habibullah when he went on his official visit to India. He had seen Bombay and Calcutta! He thought much of the English, who were wise and all-pervading, and he seemed delighted to talk to me, and astonished at my knowledge of Persian. He insisted on throwing

Wama – old man on rooftops.

away my stick, which was, he said, too heavy, and presented me instead with his own. I could not refuse this kind action, which naturally touched me. His stick is slim and strong and specially bent at the top. It was most useful on the journey, and I have it still. The final surprise about this old boy was that he had heard of Robertson! 'Oh yes,' he said, when I explained who he was, 'he was the Englishman who came down into the Parun Valley, and then there was trouble, and the people wanted to cut his throat, and he had to run away back to his country!'

We said goodbye and followed Fatty down a gentler, longer way to the bridge, while the second soldier, an Herati, who wore a white turban and always carried a big stick, complained bitterly that we were being led astray. In the end we made it, and set off over the bridge, not knowing if the others were behind or ahead of us. With us was another young Afghan, called Fateh Mohammad. He was of our party, but I had not been sure what exactly he was doing. It turned out that he was a conscript, not serving his time like Astane Gol, and the soldier with the stick, in the army, but in the police. He had been picked up by our police friends at Jalalabad as a guide for them. He was from Ghazni, and was shortly to return there when his two years had expired, to work on the telephone lines. He told me that his brother-in-law was a pilot who had trained for three years in Russia, and had been back in Afghanistan for only a year. He spoke Russian. When I asked whether he had liked it, Fateh Mohammad said that he had, but that everyone always liked the places where they studied.

It was a day of hard walking. Fatty said the porters were tired, but it was he who was tired and kept lagging behind. We had infinite difficulty choosing a good place for lunch, and in the end never found one. The country was gorgeous, with still the same fast-flowing river, and the first part of the journey was fairly consistently by its banks. I talked to the police officer, a Tajik from Charikar who, though he looked older, was only 26 and one year out of police school. He found the going a bit tough, especially since he was so totally unprepared for the journey. Once or twice we helped each other over slippery rock faces, which made for friendship. (Poor man, he has been frightened to shake hands on the odd occasion we have seen him since our return.) We also got to know the other two men about this time. Their names were Abdul Ghafur and Sardar Mohammad. They spoke highly of Kabul Radio's English lessons! (I had helped produce these with local British Council teachers, and took part myself. My peculiar accent was sometimes recognised.)

Up and down, up and down the road went on, and never seemed to get anywhere. The going became tough. We preferred to keep going steadily, though the porters preferred to go fast and have long rests. The Nuristanis are a really tough mountain people. One of our porters from Wama looked more like a boy than a man, but when we told him to go on ahead and tell JT, who was in front, to stop he complained about the weight of his load for two seconds, then disappeared from sight at a run! I wore gym shoes, which were fine at the beginning, and excellent for the treacherous going if they were kept dry, but they were hopeless, of course, in the snow later on, and on the seventh and eighth days of walking my feet got very bruised.

In the afternoon we met a travelling Safi family coming up the valley with a cow and a goat to trade with the Nuristanis. Fatty at once wanted to stop and take advantage of the food, but we told him that the others had gone on, and we could not always be changing our plans. If he came on with us (instead of lagging behind) we would let him choose a good place, we said. Of course, he did not come on. He stayed behind with Kheir Mohammad, and the two of them ate a huge meal off the poor Safis, and then came into camp terribly late.

We went on, passing the bridge that led over the river to the Kantiwar Valley. This place is called Doab. Near it are said to be the two Kantiwar villages of Umoe and Chiwad. Aspit and Chiwi are further up the valley. It is a pity we had no time to visit this valley, which could be called the heart of Nuristan, and is the home of many of her famous sons. After three-quarters of an hour we came upon Reinhard, who had gone ahead, sitting on a patch of green grass by a stream, in bliss. The country was just like his native Bavarian forests! It had suddenly changed. Birds were singing and there was a strong smell of herbs and flowers. We were entering the region of the great forests. Magnificent tall trees, mainly pine but also walnut, holly and ash, covered the slopes of the hills. Beneath them were anemones, cow parsley, a similar flower with a hot, sweet smell, bushes covered in mauve flowers, even wild roses, and many other flowers. With their scent was mingled the strong smell of thyme and other herbs. Reinhard found a superb camping spot – a grassy place with plenty of wood and a large lump of unmelted snow as a promise of things to come later. There was an island in the river, and a little pool among the rocks for us all, especially JT, to bathe in. He was a changed man once he had had a bath, and usually had two or three in the river every day! A little further on was a second level place for the others. Fatty brought up the rear, bringing the goat that he had bought from the Safi family, and would roast for all the porters and police, etc. And the family themselves turned up, with delicious dugh and mast. We had a supper out of tins, which tasted superb, and then went over to join the others, where they were roasting the

Resting in the Amhoz Valley – on the trail beyond Wama. Nicholas at left, JT centre and our translator second from right.

(rather too pregnant-looking for my liking) goat over a huge fire. Everyone was happy and contented that night, and we got a well-earned eight hours' sleep.

SATURDAY, 9 JULY

This was another day of hard walking. An hour after we left camp we came to the place called Chitras, where the Jouda Valley comes down from the east from Waigel. Where the valley meets the Pech there is a fertile spot with many fields, growing different kinds of grain. The women were working in them on their knees, hacking at the earth with sticks – they seem to have no metal implements. Occasionally one caught a glimpse of a handsome face and a flashing smile behind the heavy dark clothes that they wore. The interesting thing is that this place, although in the Pech-Parun Valley, belongs to the Waigel people from over the hill. In the days of constant warfare between tribe and tribe, it must surely have been fought over. The strong Waigel tribe won and control it now, though it is far across the mountain from their home.

At Chitras we saw our porters talking to a man in Nuristani dress who turned out to be a Safi. He took us down by the river, and showed us what he was doing. There, in a little thatched hut, he had rigged up a lathe that worked by waterpower. Where a little irrigation stream

Woman working in terraced fields.

joined the Jouda stream it was guided into a steep wooden chute. At the bottom of this chute was a wooden paddle wheel that was one end of an axle, the other end of which was in the hut and clamped to the piece of wood to be worked. The axle was supported by brackets, and the water made it turn at a brisk speed. The craftsman then attacked his lump of wood with an improvised chisel. It was all very ingenious and impressive. The fellow was making plates and big fruit bowls, and was selling them to the local Nuristanis. Most enterprising!

For lunch we came to a great strip of meadow beside the river, shaded by trees. JT arrived after us. He had found his topi too hot, given it to the little soldier Astane Gol to hold, and had tied a towel turban-wise round his own head. When the two of them arrived they

The Safi craftsman who made wooden bowls – he also came north to plant tobacco.

made a fine sight: the little soldier was wearing the topi, and the big American the turban! On a trip of this sort it is vital to have, and to wear, a hat. Perhaps a topi is the best answer. I wore a wide-brimmed summer hat of gabardine-type material, which I found quite adequate. We watched the Nuristanis playing a sort of bowls during the 'lunch break'. It was more like the French variety – they were chucking stones in the air to see who could get nearest to a small chosen stone – and they were pretty accurate at it. The most intriguing of our Nuristani porters was an old man with a yellowish beard who was dressed mainly in skins – of course, in Robertson's day this was the normal dress for many of the population. It certainly gave this old man a wild appearance. As far as I am concerned, it solved the problem of the abominable snowman! One might well think a creature like this to be an animal, and turn and run!

As we walked on after lunch, I found myself stuck with Fatty, the Sar Kateb, who was most garrulous, chiefly in an attempt to get me to go more slowly. He told me how they all feared the 'Vakil Sahib', Farouk Osman, who always looked for trouble, and never missed a thing. He thought the Hakem-e Kelan of Chigha Serai was honest too – according to him, they all had to be under Osman. He was married, but his wife was at home, in Mohmand country, and he gave the impression that he had women when he wanted to. This might have been an empty boast, like his others – but it might not. He said he was only 25 or so, much younger than he looked. He did not say anything about the Prime Minister, but he did say that he was fond of the King, and spoke highly of the King's humanity and kindness. He was very interested in our laws – about murder in the course of a family feud, for instance! If all the family egged a man on to kill someone else, were they all guilty? Not, he said, in Afghanistan. Feuds were constantly breaking out among the Safis. It took up a lot of the Hakem's time, because he had to go and try and get them to make it up, and arrange a cross-marriage of female relatives to cement the pledge of peace. He had only the vaguest of ideas about what 'Pashtunistan' was.

At half past four in the afternoon we came over a crest, and saw before us our valley of Shangri-La. It was the Parun Valley, at last. The hills had opened up and had uncovered a carpet of rich green, with the river meandering through the centre of it. The slopes on either side were still covered in dark green firs, but they were gentler than before. The valley was vivid and lush, full of willows, with myriads of streams tinkling through it. The greenness reminded me of England. It was an enchanted land, a fairy-tale land, a complete contrast to the gloomy crags of the Wamais, and when we saw the people we could have jumped for joy; they were also as unlike the tall, martial Wamais as could be – they were a little people, almost like dwarfs, but good and cheerful dwarfs. We passed a few before we came to their main village, Pashki. They were dressed in dirty white leggings and jerkins, and wore no daggers. Their eyes twinkled gaily over their lumpy little noses and their bushy black beards. They seemed very friendly, kind and simple, and utterly peaceful.

Eventually we saw Pashki itself, halfway up the hill, with its two rather prominent towers, and made our way up to the village. Pashki is 2350 metres above sea level. We were taken to a couple of spacious open roofs on the river – that is, the east – side of the village. There we established ourselves on our charpoys, drank in the view, met the no. 2 malek, drank tea and talked about the journey. One of our policemen said that, if we wanted, he could make a much better pilau than the locals. We gladly gave him our rice, instead of to the little Presuns, and were well justified – he produced a first-class meal. Eventually the no. 1 malek (by heredity, but not by personality) arrived and apologised that he had been away with his cows in the pastures. He looked exactly like one of the Seven Dwarfs – like Sleepy, in fact.

We provided tea for all after supper, and sat around talking. A rather fine-looking grey-beard in a turban was also present. He was a Munjani from over the pass in Badakhshan, and he had come to visit his daughter, who had married in Pashki. He said that he had had no difficulty in getting over the Weran Pass. He spoke a strange dialect of Persian. That was nothing, of course, to the strangeness of the Presun language itself.

The word 'Presun' itself is Kti or Kantiwari, the Presuns calling themselves Wasi. Wama they call Tsanu, which accounts for why it is so called on Robertson's map. I was told that the names of the five Presun villages in Kti were as follows: Pashki, Koshtaki, Diwe, Prontz and Ishtiwe (phonetic). In Presun language I was told that they are: Usbud, Rushud, Sutsu, Sech and Supu (ditto). It is amazing that this

Pashki malek and children.

unique language, spoken only in five villages anywhere, manages to survive.

There was much talk about the best way to get over to the Waigel Valley. We thought we might have to return to Chitras, but the Presuns said that there were passes over from these villages, so we decided to sleep on it.

SUNDAY, 10 JULY

When we woke, the sky was covered with clouds for the first time on our journey. Here and there rays from the sun were beating through,

Pashki malek and villagers.

and illuminating parts of the very green valley. We were not so high above the river as we had been at Wama, but we still had a fine view both up and down the valley, which lay below at our feet. After breakfast we asked our little head dwarf to take us round the village, and we climbed up after him through the stinking alleyways and over the roofs (often climbing from one to another by means of tree trunks with steps notched into them) until we reached the top of the village. We looked inside one house, which was used for everything, as at Wama, but which was much smaller. Below was a cellar. All these houses have cellars, which they use as a store-room, and where they live during the extreme cold of the winter, when they must often be literally snowed in. Then the animals are moved into the room above for protection too!

At the top of the village we had a closer look at one of the square towers that were a feature of the place. Another tower like the one we saw, also above the village, but on the north instead of the south side, has fallen down since the German expedition photographed it before the war. The village, too, seems to have grown since then. The towers must have originally been for defence, but now the remaining two towers are used chiefly as store places, while the one we saw also serves as the minaret for the mosque. The maleks were quite happy to show us the mosque, which consisted of a few simple rooms with wooden pillars, and also the mullah, who came along and greeted us (all the mullahs here were local, and not thought much of). We were always hoping that we might see some remnants of the old vigorous Kafir carvings of animals and men that had escaped burning, and been incorporated into someone's house; but we never did.

We prescribed – or, rather, JT prescribed – some medicine for a sick child who was some relative of the no. 2 malek, and gave presents of salt (very well received) and a special little metal cup to the head malek. Then we said our goodbyes, and wound our way down from the village, over the bridge, and on through the slushy, flowery meadows to the north. There was a pass going over to Waigel from Pashki, which we later found was probably the easiest of the many passes across the mountains, but we wanted to see something of the other villages of the Presun people, and if possible reach Ishtiwe itself.

It was a beautiful walk, gently winding alongside the river in this quite unexpectedly rich and easy valley, high up in the mountains. Robertson described it as the 'cockpit' of Nuristan, a place where all the tribes warred, and no one was safe. The Presun people themselves used to fetch and carry for the proud and warlike tribes around them, the Ramgul and Kam Katirs and the Waigel, but they still kept their valley with the best grazing in Nuristan. After an hour and a quarter we came to a tiny hamlet they called Satsum (identified later as 'Zumu', the sixth Presun village), which could not have contained more than 20 houses. It had its own malek, however, who came and talked to us. He was distinguished, as usual, by the insignia on his rough white woollen jerkin. All the maleks of the Presuns wore little designs woven into the plain white of their coats. The designs were in red and blue and consisted of small geometrical patterns, usually squares, like a chessboard, sometimes a series of small diamonds. These designs were never more than two inches square in size, and were placed on the cuff of the sleeve, or near where the lapel would be. As far as I could see, only people who were some sort of malek wore them.

The no. 2 malek of Pashki, who was taller, leaner and more intelligent-looking than his fellows, had come along with us, and stayed with us for most of the day. He had an inquiring mind, wanting to know, for example, how the aeroplanes, which were sometimes seen in the sky, worked. He was curious about the Russians and Americans, and was horrified when I made a point of telling him that the Russians believed in no god at all. He was also fairly well informed, though he could not say much about the origin of his people, except that they were supposed to have come over from the north many, many years ago. He taught me to recognise the two main types of prominent graves that we passed on the way. The highly carved, box-like graves covered in wheel or diamond patterns, and standing perhaps a foot or two high, were the graves of maleks. Some of these had unusual wooden posts with the tops curved like horses' heads driven into the ground of the grave, and leaning against the box-like wooden framework. We saw these also in the Safi country. The simple graves marked only by huge, clean knife blades of slate, sometimes 10 or 12 feet high, were the graves of holy men. He also tried to explain the queer combination of heredity and ability that decides who the maleks of the village are to be. The presumption is that son succeeds father, but energetic men who are wealthy can gradually acquire a position for themselves, and be chosen as maleks by the people. There are some people who are very wealthy, but who are not interested in outside affairs, and prefer to sit at home. These never become maleks. He was also familiar with another god not previously mentioned; this was Bagisht, the god of rivers, lakes and mountains.

I was very excited when we came to the next small village, called Koshtaki, half an hour after leaving Satsum. Koshtaki was the site of the great temple to Imra described so vividly by Robertson (on page 389 of his book), and was the most sacred village in the whole of Kafiristan. The temple as Robertson described it was 20 feet high and about 60 feet

Local grave of someone important.

square, with a portico of equal size on the east or river side. Among other things inside the temple, which was full of fine carving, were eight huge statues of Imra. Tragically, there is now nothing left of this great monument but the memory of it. Another name the Presuns use for Koshtaki is Imragram, which sounds as if it means 'the place of Imra'. They remember tales of the temple, and showed us the open stretch of ground to the north of the village where it stood. Now everything has been hacked to pieces by fanatical mullahs, the site is covered with grass, and it is difficult to visualise the vast old temple that was destroyed only 65 years ago.

We wandered up to the village mosque to see if any of the curved pillars had found their way into that building, but there was nothing

Koshtaki – most revered village in Kafiristan.

more than a few lightly carved pillars to be seen there. As far as we could discover, nothing was left. It is a great pity that almost all the unique carved figures of the old Kafirs have disappeared under the axes of the mullahs. There are comparatively very few in the Kabul museum, and the Pakistanis have now sucked dry the few villages on their side of the frontier.

We met one of the village maleks and, on the site of the old temple we sat on a rug provided by our hosts, surrounded by our dwarf companions. Koshtaki was built like the other villages up the side of the hill, but was not far from the river. When we had walked away from the village we looked back at it. Behind the village, the mountain rock rose sheer and very high, and suddenly I noticed a remarkable thing: at the

Another view of Koshtaki.

top of the mountain immediately over the village, a huge waterfall fell from the crest of the rock, one would have said straight out of the sky, 100 feet or more down a piece of rock face. Our Pashki malek escort pointed and said, 'There is Imra's water!' It did indeed look as if the god were pouring a stream of water out of the heavens, and I believe that this must have been the reason why the place was originally considered sacred, and chosen as a site for the great temple. However, I have not seen this theory mentioned by Robertson or anyone else. (Perhaps the flow was seasonal and therefore not noticed by other travellers.)

We walked on through the spongy meadows, and reached the village of Diwe at half past 12. This village was the only one we saw that was on ground level, as it were. It seemed to be built on an island in the river. Here rugs were laid out under the willow trees by a stream for our lunch, and here we decided to venture no further up the valley. If we had gone up the valley past Prontz to the last Presun village of Ishtiwe (Robertson's Shtevgrom), we should have had to come back to Diwe (Robertson's Diogrom) before trying to cross over to the Wai Valley. There are only two passes from Ishtiwi, one leads to the north-east, to Kamdesh, and the other, the Weran Pass (with a lake on either side), to the north-west, to Munjan and Badakhshan. (I learned that the most respected man in Ishtiwe, which rivals Pashki for the post of leading village of the Presuns, is a certain Mazamer Khan, who is a merchant now in Kabul.) So we decided to go as far as we could up the pass to the east that we were told led to the Wai Valley, so that we could get over the next day. We knew we had a tough climb ahead of us.

Lunch at Diwe.

Before we set off for the Kotal (mountain pass) we said goodbye to our garrulous, scurrilous guide – the Sar Kateb (Fatty). We had become almost fond of him, and were sorry to say goodbye to him. He had no intention of exerting himself by crossing the pass. We also had to say goodbye to the old white-bearded porter. Though he was game, I believe the others said that he should not attempt the ascent. We also had to engage new porters from Diwe to carry us over the top, since the Pashki porters were going back with their malek. This proved quite difficult, and we suffered many delays before we finally distributed bakhsheesh to the people who were leaving us and set off up a gully into the mountain.

On leaving Diwe, our malek friend talked to a rather beautiful unveiled girl who was working in the fields. This was his daughter, who had married someone from Diwe. They have the reputation of being free and easy in relations between the sexes in the Parun Valley. We were told that men and women actually danced together, and that they also drank wine, but we never saw any proof of either of these statements. Eventually, after more porter trouble (two of them had stayed behind to have a meal), we reached the end of the cultivated area, where we said goodbye and thank-you to our kind malek escort and I gave him a torch, a present with which he seemed delighted. Then we were off, in a long-drawn-out string of men, for the unknown mountains.

We wound up a steep gully, walking on the stale, dirty snow that was lying in it unmelted. A small stream rushed down underneath the snow, forming great caverns that were visible here and there when the stream came to the surface.

Walking in the snow was difficult. Up and up we went, over all sorts of terrain, the Nuristani porters, strong and stocky, leading the way at a good, fast pace. We usually saw to it that one of the three of us was up in front with the leaders. Eventually, as the sun was going down, we crossed a slope of snow and came to a small grassy patch beside the stream, where there was a hut belonging to some Diwe people who were up looking after the cows in the higher pasture. We decided to stop, since the place was protected, and we could get fresh mast and curds from the people. The man in charge (later given eye ointment by

Beginning of a glacial snow patch.

JT) seemed a bit uneasy, but we put up our big tent on the only suitable flat space near the little bridge.

It was going to be chilly during the night, so we let the translator and the police have Reinhard's small tent, and laid out our beds in the big tent, which took three without much difficulty. We began to cook ourselves a meal, and the people from the stone hut brought us excellent mast and dugh, and also milk and admirable butter and curds (which taste like cream cheese). Then, suddenly, we saw why our host had been worried. The cows began to come back from further up the little valley and paused, frightened, when they saw our tent right in their traditional path to the bridge and their resting place. Before we knew what was happening, one cow had made a dash for it, skipping over the tent ropes, pulling some out of the ground and causing a small tear in the fabric of the tent. Disaster! We all rose, armed with sticks, and tried to shoo the cows up the hill and round some rocks – a more circuitous path to the bridge. It was not easy. The cows had fixed ideas about where they wanted to go, and they were coming more and more, perhaps 30 or 40 of them. Eventually, our officer called out his policemen. And then we had the splendid spectacle of three uniformed Kabul policemen, way up in the Hindu Kush, trying to protect a tent from a troupe of truculent cows! They worked very well (it was about the only time that the police were directly useful to us!), and after some excitement the cows got home. These cows, like all the cows we saw in Nuristan, were well kept and well fed. With barley bread, their products supply the basic diet of the people. Fat products are one of the few exports that leave the valleys in exchange for the tea, sugar and matches that the people need. The sky darkened as if a storm were brewing up, so we weighted the tent round with stones, and went to bed.

MONDAY, 11 JULY

It was bitterly cold when we awoke and washed in the icy stream. We left camp for the long climb to the top and over at 6:30 a.m., and we put on our sweaters and wind jackets. Soon we came to a high plateau, green and brilliant with flowers. I have not seen an Alpine meadow, but I was told this was similar. The air was bracing, the sky blue, and the path underfoot was lush and green. Sometimes we were knee-deep in undergrowth. Flowers of all sorts were everywhere, and in particular we passed examples of every type of rock plant I have ever seen. Later we came to acres of wild rhubarb, which we gathered and I stewed for supper. It was quite delicious.

Occasionally we passed convenient slate benches, and here we rested and recuperated from the climb. The first time we did this, four of the porters from Diwe got together and started to sing. Accompaniment was provided by one of the fellows banging one stick against another. The song was a sort of shout with a refrain, but a tuneful one, and it had several parts, making a sort of harmony. It was also very gay and

The glacier begins. Note the tent at the edge of an ice pack.

cheerful, and the porters who were standing in a circle with their loads still on began to jig in time to the singing. One young fellow started to twirl and raise his arms in a dance.

Watching them was an exciting and invigorating experience. They obviously thoroughly enjoyed themselves, and were refreshed by their exertions. Later we got to know these porters quite well, for they stayed with us for two and a half days. They were a bit argumentative, but very easy and natural, besides being cheerful – not a bit servile. I remember particularly a young redhead, tough and silent, who was always in the lead; also a stout man, who carried the heavy weight of two tents. He used to complain about his leg, and had JT examine it. We saw that there were great scars where people had applied local remedies by burning

Porters taking a break.

the knee with red-hot coals, but there was nothing we could do. It did not seem to stop the old fellow from going like a bomb. Then there was the young dancer, whose name was Qadar Jan, and who was a most talkative and inquisitive youth with blondish hair. He had just married, but did not seem worried about leaving his wife. Most Nuristanis are famous for their filth, but Qadar Jan was always begging soap off us so that he could wash his clothes. Then there was the oldish man who we called 'Diwane', or 'madman'. He had a heart-shaped black beard, and acted (or was) rather foolish, but he was an excellent singer.

As we climbed, we came to some more stone buildings for the use of the animals. Around on neighbouring hills I noticed some upright stones silhouetted, looking just like men. I was told that they were

View from the ascent to the Drumgul Pass.

meant to do so, and thereby to scare off would-be thieves. Eventually we came to the snow, and then the going became very hard. Up and up we climbed, till all the surrounding mountains were suddenly visible – great peaks covered with snow, extending one after another into the distance. The rare air made the going even more difficult. We reckoned that we were at an altitude of about 15,000 feet on the top of the Kotal. After some hard climbing, we found ourselves at the foot of a long, glacier-like approach to the col. We were very strung out now, and it took us a great deal of time before we finally trudged up the last steep, treacherous snow slope to the pile of stones that marked the crest. Mountains rose up on either side, and we saw our snowy path extending way down into the valley before us. In the meantime, we threw ourselves exhausted on the stones. I was tempted to use a phrase from my self-made Nuristani phrase book, 'Pron bo-dreigha bo-chum ahiew', which means 'The road is long and steep' (verb at the end, of course). Then the silent redheaded Presun porter from Diwe produced a simple flute, and the gentle sound of triumph echoed around the mountaintops. Justifiable triumph was the feeling of everyone as they made the top, one after the other. Soon people started clapping their hands, and old Diwane got up and did a sort of belly dance. Then little Astane Gol also felt the urge to dance and took the girl's part, dancing provocatively in front of him with much movement of the hips. The police officer's uniform was looking very much the worse for wear, but he was the hero of the hour, for in a sustained burst of energy he had been the first to reach the top. (I think I was second.)

Drumgul pass over the col.

Then we went down, one after another, down the steep slippery slope to the east. The three policemen went down in a little group on their backsides, looking like something out of the silent films. As the slope flattened out, we came to the most treacherous part of all. The snow was melting in the midday sun, and we began to fall down through it time and time again, sometimes up to our knees, sometimes up to our waists and further. It was hilariously funny, and dangerous at the same time; hilariously funny when other people suddenly disappeared from view below the snow, dangerous when one fell oneself. Once, when I fell through the snow four times in ten paces, I almost gave up trying, but eventually we got clear on to rocky ground, and then at last the snow was gone. The droppings of animals had helped us trace the route over the pass. The people take the animals over at night when the snow is frozen hard (cows, sheep and goats); they could not, of course, ever take them over in the daytime because they would surely fall through as we did, and be maimed. They take huge torches of burning twigs to see them across. They go across because, strange though it is, the high pastures in the upper end of the Waigel Valley belong to the Presuns. The village of Diwe has three 'Bandars' over the Kotal, the centre one of which we eventually came to. To the south, Koshtaki villagers have one Bandar. The other villages have their Bandars to the east of their villages on the other side of the Parun river. The Afghans call 'Bandar' what the Persians, using a Turkish word, call 'Yeilaq', meaning 'summer quarters' or the place in the mountains to which the men and the flocks move during the summer months.

As we came down the other side, we passed again through Alpine meadow scenery. In one particular place we came upon acres of violets. It was a little further down that we heard a repeated and persistent screech from somewhere in the valley. Eventually we saw what it was. It was monkeys. Quite big ones, of a chestnut brown colour. But they did not allow us to get very near. The police officer went off after them with his pistol, but had no luck. These were the only wild animals that we saw in Nuristan, though we knew that there were quite a few bears (black and brown, according to Thesiger), as well as leopards and mountain goats and ibex, to be found.

Eventually we could see the Wai Valley itself. We had come in right at the end of it. To our left was an impressive wall of mountains;

opposite, another difficult pass led from the Wai Valley over to the area of Kamdesh; to our right the Wai river itself disappeared between the mountains on its long way down to join the Pech by Manugai. We came upon the Bandar quite suddenly. We walked down through a steep bit of greenery with so many bushes and flowers that it looked like a public park specially laid out; then we suddenly saw in front of us an ancient yew tree, and beneath it, on the crest of the ridge we were on, three little stone huts. About 15 or 20 men and boys of all ages, in their thick, dirty white clothes, came out and welcomed us with a sort of symbolic hug on both sides. Foremost of them was a smallish man with a face of great character, reddish hair and twinkling eyes, and with the usual insignia on his jerkin – this was our host for the night, the local malek. This Bandar was under his control. We learned later that the next one higher up the Wai Valley was under the biggest malek of the village, and one of the richest and most devout men in the Parun Valley, malek Baz Mohammad. (They said he had 60 cows, more than anyone else in the valley. Our local malek had 13.)

The view was very fine. The ridge we were on was very green and covered with flowers, mostly tall white flowers looking rather like hyacinths, but it fell steeply away each side from a narrow 'back'. We could follow it clearly falling away in front of us down to the river, a mile or two below, to a place where other valleys and ridges converged. On the steep slopes opposite lived the Gujers, a wandering people, presumably Indian in origin, found all over eastern Afghanistan. (Gujers are one of the main sub-tribes in the Punjab – thus the towns Gujranwala and Gujer Khan in Pakistan. The hill people seem to be a gypsy-like offshoot of their settled cousins.) There is a large concentration of them near Asmar. They have been increasing in recent years. Our malek obviously disliked them intensely, because they had gradually been encroaching on pastures traditionally belonging to his people, and also because they were thieves of cattle and other things. He even tried to get our police officer to go and shoot some of them further down the valley! It would be interesting to find out more about the Gujers in Afghanistan.

It was about half past three. Our two Safi porters, the brothers, were sick. One had fever and was given penicillin. We had a sheep slaughtered for food for our party (it was done ritually and rather horribly), had a

The Bandar – stone sleeping huts.

cup of tea, and then looked around for a place for the tent. We almost decided we would have to move on because there was no flat place, except for the mud roofs of their stone huts. But at last we found a patch of grass that was not too violently sloped, and accepted the malek's offer to have it levelled out a bit. Some men came along, but they had no tools. They broke off bits of slate and used them to scratch at the earth. The little job took some time, but eventually the tent was up. The Herati soldier with the stick (his name was Sadruddin) obligingly went down to a clear stream 100 yards below to get us some water to wash in. While walking I always took good care to see that he was not walking behind me, because he had the infuriating habit of treading on one's heels. This quality of his, however, made him splendidly fitted to bring up the stragglers in any column, a job that was invariably assigned to him. Our tent was a little way from the old yew tree and the main hut, and the soldier insisted on curling up on the ground outside, as always, to guard us, though we tried to persuade him to find somewhere in the warm.

Once we were clean and organised, we went up the hill to join the crowd sitting round a huge pot on the fire outside the main hut, in which the rest of the sheep was being boiled. Part of it had been roasted for us as kebab, and this we ate, together with the locally made barley bread. We asked if they would sing for us, and Qader Jan told me to ask the malek, who was the best singer of the lot, which I did. With his bright little eyes twinkling he agreed, and, taking an upturned saucepan and a spoon, he began to lead the others in several songs. Someone in the background had a simple guitar. The singing was full and warm and seemed much closer to Western music than the music of India or Persia. The malek led, a black-beard sitting next to him followed, and the rest took up the refrain. There, high up on the ridge, with the glow of the fire reddening the bearded little faces of our hosts, and with the music swelling out from the fireside, the occasion was unforgettable – the most memorable of all the memories of our journey.

The Presuns were absorbed in the songs and so were we. After a time Qader Jan and some of the others could not resist the call of the music, and started to dance in a little dusty space cleared by the fire. As the song rose and fell, they shuffled their feet in the peculiar set step to which they dance, and began to move their arms, clap their hands and twirl around inside the circle. Perhaps there were five or six of them. Robertson has a good description of a Presun dance on page 119 of his book. The night was black, and the only light was from the fire and a few rude torches held up by juniors in the circle. As the singers got worked up, so did the dancers, and the dust flew, while the dark shapes twisted and turned in front of us. We asked what the songs were about, and were told that they were about the martial legends of the past, the days when the Kafirs used to go down the valleys and proudly come back with the scalps of the 'Mussulmans'. When we asked the malek if he could sing us a love song, the dancers stopped, and all concentrated intently on the great artist. He sang with another, our old friend Diwane, if I remember right, and the two put on a wonderful series of facial expressions depicting love and coquetry between man and woman. Then as the song developed the malek got more and more carried away, and leaving the accompaniment to another he started to wave his arms about, and then slowly rose from his place and moved into the circle, where he began to jerk his body about in a fantastically expressive dance. His eyes were staring, and as he got more excited one could see that the dance was very definitely erotic in meaning. After a bit some of the others became worried, worried perhaps lest he should lose control completely, and took hold of him and made him sit down. His eyes were still staring, and he was quite possessed. We faded away tactfully with murmurs of appreciation, and went to bed.

Dancing – continuing traditions of the past – out of sight of the mullahs.

TUESDAY, 12 JULY

We were all up early this day, but Reinhard and I had to stay behind until the tents dried in the sun before we could pack them up and leave. When everything was ready we thanked the little malek, gave him some salt and other presents, and set off down the hill. The malek confirmed what I thought: that no other Europeans or foreigners had ever come across the particular pass that we had crossed. He had seen no strangers in all his years. I had read no accounts of such a crossing. It felt good to be, in some tiny way, a pioneer. We soon reached the Wai river and spent the rest of the day in an arduous walk, following its interminable twists and turns, until we finally reached the village of Waigel, chief place of the Waigel tribe. It was at this stage of the journey that our bodies began to crack up under the strain. We started to suffer from burnt arms and faces and mashed feet. We gave ourselves a much-needed treat by finishing off a tin of pineapple for lunch in a little fly-ridden glade under some ash trees near the river. We also helped ourselves – or rather, JT issued us with – an extra helping of Tang, the wonderful American powder that produces a vitamin-filled fruit juice when mixed with water. In fact, during the whole trip we could not speak too highly of Tang. We made up slogans in its praise as we went along: 'Tang for tired travellers' or 'Take a Tang – you'll soon long for another taste of Tang'. In the early part of the day we passed through dark pinewoods and little settlements of Gujers and other people. Later we came to the Bandars of the Waigel tribe themselves, distinguished by their prosperous bearing and steep pointed roofs open to the air at the ends (perhaps for storing grain?).

Later still we came to real Waigel settlements, first small strips of cultivated land by the river. The Waigel have always been famous for their good qualities – their bravery, hospitality and beauty, among other things. Certainly, we passed on the road some lovely girls only half veiled, and some striking-looking men. The Waigel tend to have thin, finely moulded faces similar to, but more aristocratic, than the faces of the Wamais. They are also well built, but we never saw a fat Nuristani anywhere, and only one or two undernourished ones. The prosperity of the place was also noticeable – all the houses seemed to be newly repaired and touched up. There had been no houses like that in Wama or in the Parun Valley.

As we walked south, dead exhausted, the valley became greener and more intensely cultivated, and at about 5:00 p.m., after 11 hours on the road, we came near the village of Waigel itself. We were met by children, who ran off to give the word, then by a soldier in uniform sent from the Hokumati and finally by two brothers, who turned out to be the maleks of the upper village. We were escorted thus to a space below the village, shaded by some trees, where three magnificently caparisoned charpoys were set out in a hollow square for our benefit after we had passed through a reception committee of welcoming grey-beards. We greeted

Goats grazing, on route down to the Wai river.

Waigel huts and shepherds.

the Kotowal Sahib from the Hokumati down the valley, who was looking plump and pleased that we had appeared after all, and also a slim middle-aged man, who looked intelligent and who was treated with great respect by the people. He was called the 'Vakil Sahib'. We flung ourselves on to our beds and thankfully drank tea that was prepared – the first time that we had not had to make it ourselves. It was obvious that we were going to be well looked after.

We were resting below the lower village (the young malek of which was away). Through the trees to the east we could see the houses of the upper village clinging like limpets to their rock the other side of a gorge. That was where the two brother maleks ruled (one of whom was sitting by us on a chair dressed in a sports coat with a loud check), but the maleks deferred to the Vakil Sahib, who had been, as his name implied, at one time a member of parliament for the area. Various tribes take turns to have the seat in the House of Deputies, and this man (who is a big landowner, because his father became a Hakem somewhere in Afghanistan, and bought up the land on his retirement), held the seat for three years some time before, and consequently knew Kabul and the big wide world well. But, although our host was familiar with Kabul, he was also most interested in Nuristan itself and his own tribe. He gave us the information about the passes between the Waigel and Pech-Parun Valleys that is contained in the map, and he told us theories about the origin of his tribe. He also told us that there were 2000 people living in the two villages of Waigel, and a total of 6000 to 7000 people living in the whole

Waigel. Exhausted, we meet with village elders. (Nicholas at left. JT on right.)

valley (which makes that the total of the tribe). Also that since the King's visit a year or so ago a school had been installed at Waigel, and teachers had come in from outside for certain months in the year. Persian and Pashtu reading and writing were the only subjects taught in fact. He also told us about the old days, when Waigel raiding parties would go down the valley to murder Muslims for fun, and when small boys from their earliest infancy were brought up to kill others.

We found that the police had taken a nearby roof for their beds, and that we had been assigned the village public place at which we had tea. We were not satisfied with this, thinking that the police were pulling a fast one, and soon had the police turfed out, and ourselves installed in their stead. We had more privacy on our roof, except for one thing: during the night I became the public property of a legion of bedbugs, which munched me all over, despite lavish shakings of DDT. I am told that the cure for these obnoxious insects, which live in the beds themselves, is to bury the whole bed for three days to suffocate them. I hope they did that to my bed before too many others suffered, but as a guest it was hardly my place to suggest it.

Near our roof was a private path down to the river, and a large bucket of hot water was placed down there for our ablutions. We had an excellent shave and bath, and appeared up in the clearing refreshed and with a good strong appetite. This mounted as we watched the young blades of the village do a warrior dance. It took some time to get the young men together. A small three-piece band (two flutes and a drum) played to call everyone to come and take part. The men came in driblets, all carrying a long, unsheathed sword. These, like the daggers invariably worn by all Waigel men (and all Wamais), have been passed down from father to son, and are jealously preserved. We examined one or two, but could not discover their age or origin. There was fine workmanship in them. When 12 or 15 of the men were gathered together they began the dance, under the direction of an energetic young man in a red shirt. They moved round in a circle with special steps, sometimes hopping sideways, sometimes walking straight, shaking their feet in time to the music, and occasionally all rushing into the centre and shouting what sounded like an aggressive guttural battle cry: 'Whu-ooh'. Not all the youths knew the dance, because they had to be drilled by the red-shirted choreographer by means of the blowing of a whistle (rather unromantic and out of key), and the dance was a bit monotonous, for it never varied throughout the evening, as far as I could see, which made me think it was a comparatively recently inspired revival of an old dance. But the effect was still powerful, as the circling gallants went round faster and faster with their swords upright in their hands, and their forearms parallel with the ground. I fancy that this sort of dance would have been danced by the old Kafirs after their murderous forays. It would have been a dance to Gish, the god of war (see Robertson, page 616). I asked the Vakil Sahib when this dance was danced, and he replied that, except for honouring special visitors, the village danced it on certain fixed days in the year. He did not know why the days were chosen, but he agreed with me that they must coincide with the old Kafir festivals. While the dance was in progress, the small band of pipes and drums processed round the outside of the circle.

When supper came we were ready for it. Behind us a large spread was laid out – masses of bread, soup and deliciously cooked chicken provided for us by our host. The vast array disappeared in next to no time. I bolted my food in a disgusting fashion to try and keep up. After supper there was more dancing, but it was the same dance again, and after talking to the Vakil Sahib and a Mohmand trader who was temporarily doing business in the village, we excused ourselves and went to bed. As we fell asleep the dance was still continuing and figures with drawn swords were still flashing around in the torchlight.

WEDNESDAY, 13 JULY

In the morning we distressed our escort by wanting to see something of the village instead of starting straightaway. In the end the porters went on ahead with Kheir Mohammad, our translator. We stayed for a tour of the village with the Vakil Sahib, seeing some of the fine carving done on the doors of the houses (which were flat-roofed – only the odd single house by itself in the fields ever had a sloping roof), and having a surreptitious look at the people themselves. Most of them wore the Chitrali hat and the traditional thick trousers, but some wore

Waigel – traditionally ornamented door carving.

Western-type jackets. A high proportion of them (I should say perhaps 20%) were very fair indeed, and could have passed in Europe as German or Scandinavians. They had blond hair, blue eyes and a light complexion (on the whole, Nuristanis have the same varied shades of complexion that the Afghans have). We met no surly looks. The Waigel lived up to their reputation of hospitality, and all of them seemed happy to see us. We were shown a bow and arrow, and one man made a tolerably accurate demonstration of shooting with it. They still use the bow and arrow all over Nuristan for hunting. We asked to see their family daggers. One was produced for JT, and he bought it, so I offered to do the same, and a man watching rushed into his hut and produced his. They were fearfully expensive – valued at the cost of something like two and a half sheep! That is how the price was calculated.

When we finally left the village at about 8:30 a.m., we came upon all the grey-beards again, sitting waiting to say goodbye to us at the other end of the village. We shook hands with each and every one of them and set off accompanied for a full hour by the Vakil Sahib himself, out of traditional courtesy. We had given him some good presents. He had really been very kind to us, and we were very grateful to him.

We had a long, hard day's walking, and even by 7:00 p.m. did not get to within striking distance of the Hokumati at Manugai, our goal. The Kotowal Sahib guided us along the tricky and sometimes dangerous path near the torrential river, in preference to the easy but tedious path that runs right along the top of the mountains. Occasionally we caught glimpses of buildings way up at the top of the mountains; such a place, for instance, was Bandash.

I remember two major incidents on the journey. The first was where the path by the river ended in a wall of smooth rock. The Kotowal Sahib thought for a bit and then said, 'Over there,' pointing up the rock, and helped us up after him. There followed a stretch of about 100 yards of real climbing – toeholds and finger-holds in the smooth rock – that was exhilarating but not easy. Our Safi porters rushed past us, sticking to the rock like flies by some remarkable feat of balance and helping the weaker brethren. To the surprise of us all, and to the great relief of our plump little Kotowal Sahib, we made it. None of us, however, will forget the experience, for which we were quite unprepared.

The second incident occurred when I was walking with someone some 200 yards ahead of JT and another party. We had just crossed a rather tricky bit of rock, climbing close above the water, when my companion pointed to the river and gasped. There, floating down the river at a colossal rate, was a stick that I knew, and my companion knew, to be JT's. I turned in alarm, half expecting to see JT himself floating down after his stick, imagining horrible things, then saw to my relief that he was safe and following after us. It turned out that he had thrown his stick forward so that it would not impede him, and it had slipped into the water. But I had had a real fright. We had heard a tragic story the day before of how a child had fallen into the river recently, and the body had been found near Lalpura, below Jalalabad, just 12 hours later.

Although the going was easier as we went south, we still could not reach our goal, and were forced to spend a night out under the stars by the river, opposite a small settlement called Yan that was the most northerly settlement of Safis up the valley. There was a dangerous single-pole bridge over to the settlement, and two sure-footed Nuristanis borrowed a hurricane lamp to go across and bring back food for the porters.

THURSDAY, 14 JULY

On our final morning we were up and off at 6:00 a.m., having drunk Alka Seltzer to settle our long-suffering stomachs. We soon came to a difficult piece of rock-climbing that made us grateful that we had not

End of the trail. The three of us pictured together, at last. From left: Nicholas, JT and Reinhard

tried to go on in the dark the previous night. We reached the Hakem's house in two hours' quick walking without stops, but although we had sent on someone to warn him we found it empty. So, we went round to the south end of the village, and saw that the Hakem was holding court, and dealing with cases brought to him by the people. We first greeted our driver and assured ourselves that the cars were all right; then we went over to the Hakem, interrupted his business for a second, and went and sat down at his side. Milk and the tasty sweet bread were brought for us. We met and talked to two other dignitaries of the little local government; the police commandant or Zabet, with bristling moustaches and bristling ammunition belt, and the very impressive and immaculate young Qazi, or judge. He was Kabul-trained, and had been serving in this Hokumat of Darre Pech for a couple of years. It had been his first outside assignment. He was a striking figure because of the spotless whiteness of his clothes, in such contrast to the surrounding petitioning tribesmen – an ideal subject for a Persil advertisement. He was also well informed and intelligent, and must have been intellectually frustrated in this remote little post.

When all the party was gathered in we said goodbye to the Hakem and his officials, leaving them at their work, and after loading our vehicles said a final and sad farewell to our companions on the trip. We handed out pay, tips and suitable presents, and all seemed content – so little is required to satisfy them. We said goodbye to our faithful Safi porters, who had come the whole trip with us, to our soldiers Astane Gol and Sadruddin, and to our friend the Kotowal Sahib. We did not say goodbye to the police until we parted from them at Jalalabad, nor to our translator till we dropped him near his home in Kabul that night.

2 Report on the Sefid Posh

Joseph T. Kendrick
US embassy, Kabul
1960

Background on the tribes visited, including topography, houses, economy, dress, administrative structure, religion, roles of the women, health, etc.

MAIN GROUPS

The tribes of Kafiristan or Nuristan are traditionally divided into the Siah Posh (the Black Robes) and the Sefid Posh (the White Robes). These names were derived from the dark-coloured raiment that the Siah Posh wear, as distinguished from the light-coloured wool cloth worn by the Sefid Posh. Even Robertson uses this classification, but he acknowledges that is it not entirely correct. Today among the tribes of the Pech and Waigel, normally those referred to as Sefid Posh, the terms are no longer in use, although they are faintly remembered. For convenience, however, the tribes of the Pech and Waigel will be referred to in this account as the Sefid Posh. Actually, the Sefid Posh refer to all the Siah Posh tribes as Katirs, whom they regard as being of one stock linguistically and ethnographically. Outside this group they list four major peoples who, although they have different languages and are only vaguely akin among themselves, are nonetheless closer to them than to the Katirs. These four tribes, which can be considered the Sefid Posh, are:

1. Presuns – who are settled along the Pech river from the Jouda north to the end of the Pech near the ridge of the Hindu Kush. They also have grazing rights over the Drumgul Pass into the upper Waigel.

2. Wais – who are settled from about two-thirds up the Waigel southwards to within about two kilometres of where the river joins the Pech at Ningrelam. The Wais also occupy the Jouda Valley all the way to the Pech. (A small strip between the Wais and the Presuns along the Waigel river has been taken over by nomadic Gujers, who graze their livestock here during the summer but return to the upper Kunar Valley near Asmar for the winter.)

3. Wamaites – who occupy the Pech from Safi territory at the Safrigal river to the Jouda, where, after a few Wai settlements along the Jouda Valley on the east bank, there begins Presun territory.

4. Ashkuns – who are settled on a tributary that enters the Kantiwar river from the south. They, therefore, are in the area to the west of the Wamaites. The Wamaites and Ashkuns are regarded as being very closely related and possibly of the same stock. (We saw no Ashkuns on our trip.)

Relations of the various Sefid Posh tribes both among themselves and with the Katirs appear to be good, and there is considerable intermarriage between them.

TOPOGRAPHY

The country occupied by the Sefid Posh stretches from high Alpine lands of deep pine forests and green meadows, at times even going above the timber line, to deep, tortuous valleys and ravines covered with holly oak towards the south. Small, icy mountain streams pick up in volume until they become raging torrents as they rush to the lowlands. Separating the main valleys are rugged and snow-capped mountain ranges of considerable altitude. Many of the upper narrow valleys hold their glaciers and snowfields all year round. During the winter the passes become snow-blocked and leave the few villages isolated from each other.

The area between the Pech and Waigel Valleys is rugged and mountainous but is broken by several passes, which permit communication during the summer between the two areas. The northernmost passes lead over snowfields. The passes over the mountains are, from south to north: Nishaie, Yemamesh, Amshos (near Wama), Chitras (Jouda Valley), Birgul, Saman, Satsum (near Pashki) and Drumgul (near Diwe).

PHYSICAL CHARACTERISTICS

No general description of the physical features of the Sefid Posh can be given, for they are of several distinctive racial stocks. The picture is further confused by the fact that there have undoubtedly been intermarriage and influxes, resulting in a dilution of whatever original characteristics any particular tribe may have had. This is particularly true of the complexion of the members of a tribe, for each tribe has both light- and dark-complexioned people, not one colour to the exclusion of the other. Despite these limitations, however, the party did leave with a few impressions of the physical features of the Sefid Posh, such as the prominence of the aquiline features and absence of Tartar or Mongolian traits. All move with agility and can carry tremendous loads with rapidity and little difficulty over their mountainous terrain. The Wamaites, who claim to be of Arabic origin, are generally tall with long, thin faces. Their skin is swarthy, although some have a light complexion. The Presuns are very short in stature (below five feet). Beyond this, they resemble Nordic fishermen. A large percentage of light-complexioned men are also to be seen among the Presuns. The Waigelis, with the complexion of soft bronze, resemble southern Europeans, particularly Italians. Their bone structure is delicate and fine.

VILLAGES AND HOUSES

Virtually all Sefid Posh villages are built with a view to their strategic location and protection. They are built on the slopes of hills, so access

Two porters on the trail. Typical Nuristanis.

On the trail along the Pech River, keeping clear of the torrent.

Children watching from Wama rooftops. Houses stacked like steps.

The young No. 1 malek of Wama.

above Wama terrace
overlooking the Pech
River and the valley
from which we had
arrived. Our
amazing resting
place. Notice our
police officer at
centre right.

left Cheerful porter,
happy to pose.

Old man along the Pech.

Woman carrying a great cone of wood, protecting her face from a picture.

Valley in the upper Pech region.

above Travelling
towards the
Parun Valley.
The vegetation
began to change.

left Looking towards
the Parun Valley.

Pashki village – upper and lower levels.

Pashki malek.

Malek No. 2 crossing bridge below Pashki.

Malek and daughter outside Diwe.

At last a view of the elusive faces of some women.

Crossing the river and leading up to the glacier. Note river emerging at bottom below the ice pack.

Spontaneous dancing among the porters on the hard road in the col.

Approach to the col.

above Top of the
world – 'road is long
and steep'.

left Malek of the
high Bandar where
we spent the night.
Note the insignia on
his coat sleeve.

View from Diwe Bander camping space. Looking towards the route down to the Waigel Valley.

Young men of Waigel – note more European dress.

above Grave of a malek.

left Climbing along precipitous cliff along the river. Not out of trouble yet.

Dagger from Waigel associated with passage to manhood.

is normally quite difficult. They are made of different combinations of wooden beams, mud and stones. The roofs are flat and the roof of one house forms the street of the house above it, but, since the houses are staggered up the hillside, the level of the street changes abruptly. Some of the houses are two or three storeys high. The trail from one elevation to another may sometimes take advantage of the cliff for a way up to the next layer of houses, but at other times a large log hewed for steps serves as the ladder. Almost without exception the doors contain beautiful carved designs. They are smooth and black with smoke and age, and have obviously been handed down for generations. The smoke escapes through a simple hole in the roof, or into a chimney, a cube of about four feet, which protrudes above the roof. This type of chimney is particularly found among the Presuns. Some of the lower floors of the houses have porches about six feet wide, which hang over the valley. Some houses have a large window, which overlooks the valley below. In some of the villages the houses on the lower slopes are used as quarters for the cattle and sheep.

The rooms of the houses are low, usually about seven to ten feet. The roof is supported by several columns of carved designs. In the centre is a small pit for the fire, above which is usually the only cooking utensil. Water is carried in wooden buckets, gourds or clay pots. Food is taken with the hands. A crude felt or black and white woven rug, locally made, covers part of the wooden floor. Nothing was seen that might have served as a lamp or light at night other than torches. The only other items of furniture are a charpoy (a low bed – although obviously some sleep on the floor) and a number of small stools about a foot high and covered with rawhide leather. No dining tables were seen. The Presun rooms are black and dirty, as though they are caves. In Waigel village, however, the rooms are clean and have a light, airy atmosphere. In addition to the above, the Wais have low chairs, brightly painted, and with rawhide seats, resembling very much Mexican chairs.

DRESS

The dress of the Sefid Posh is distinctive by its coarse white wool cloth, used for both trousers and jackets. Although the same material is used by all the tribes, there is some variation in style. The Wamaites and Wais wear trousers, which end slightly below the knees. The calves of the leg are then thickly wrapped, to give added strength in climbing the mountains, with black cloth strips as leggings about two inches wide. The effect is to give their legs a grotesque appearance. Presumably because the Presuns live in more level terrain but in a higher and colder climate, they have modified the dress, so that their trousers are full length and wide at the ankles but are wrapped around the calves by a string. The Presuns wear a waist-length jacket made of the same material as the trousers. The jacket has a number of embroidered designs, which resemble the patterns of the carved woodwork. Very few of the jackets were seen among the Wais or Wamaites, but they had little need to protect themselves against the cold in the month of July, whereas the Presuns did.

There are variations in their footwear. The Wamaites and a few Presuns wear moccasins of goatskin. The Wais have a better moccasin, which seems to be of deerskin. Most of the Presuns, much poorer than their neighbours, go barefoot. All three tribes use the Chitrali caps. None seems to have a distinctive shirt but use crude cotton or woollen shirts, which are obviously imported. Both the Wamaites and Wais wear the wide studded belt and the Nuristani dagger with the deep, double-cross iron handle, six-to-eight inch blade and sheath ornamented with brass studs. Although the red kerchief tied around the neck is commonly used among the West Katirs, only one Sefid Posh was noticed wearing the kerchief. Most men wear a beard, although some of the younger men are clean-shaven.

DIET

It was difficult to determine exactly what the normal diet of the Sefid Posh might be. They seem to grow no vegetables except corn, which they use as animal fodder. They have no tea, sugar, salt or rice. Fruits are not abundant, although there are some apricots, walnuts and mulberries. They seem to exist largely on nan (local unleavened bread), curds, cheese and a roshan made from the fat of the sheep. Occasionally this is supplemented by chickens, eggs or mutton. They eat fish but appear to catch only a few, because they use only their hands, no hooks or nets. In the pasturelands they have milk, mast (local yoghurt), dugh and butter. On two occasions, however, we had hints that they still make a wine. The Kafirs were known in the past for their strong wines and bacchanalian orgies. We were given no wine, however, and except near Waigel village we saw no vineyards. Of the grains, they grow wheat, barley and millet. No rain cultivation was seen, and all crops are grown on terraced plots irrigated by small ditches leading from the river or one of the side streams. Once on the middle Pech we were told by a Safi that he was growing tobacco. However, the Nuristanis do not seem to grow tobacco. They keep sheep, goats and cattle, but no horses were observed.

HEALTH

The Sefid Posh appear to be quite healthy, although it is obvious that they have their share of ailments. There is no doctor in either the Pech or Waigel, and the old hakims (traditional herbal medicine doctors) still seem to continue their practices. One young man asked us to do something for his leg. During a fall some months past he had apparently pulled a tendon, and it had continued to hurt. When we looked at it, we saw a mass of still partly burned marks where the hakims had placed red-hot coals against his leg in an effort to draw out the pain. We declined to touch the case. The one ailment so common in other parts of Afghanistan, dysentery, does not seem to bother these people. The thing that they do have great trouble with, though, is eye disease. As a protective measure they wear a red solution around their eyes; the medication tends to give them a hollow and emaciated look. Some children we saw had head sores, but most appeared very healthy, especially those in the Bandars. The smaller children are usually taken to the high pasturelands by their fathers during the summertime. There they have access to dairy products, and in general live in a healthful environment.

THE WOMEN

In the olden days the Nuristani women living in their border regions were reputed to be among the most beautiful in the world, and were preyed upon by their Muslim neighbours as prizes for slavery or to be their brides. While this practice has ceased, the women still have a reputation for their beauty. On the more realistic side, they are the beasts of burden, childbearers and cultivators. Sometimes an older woman in the village looks after several children. But at 4:30 in the morning, as dawn is breaking, the younger women, often with children in their arms, leave the village for the fields in the valley below. When taken to the fields, the children are left in a corner of the plot where the mother is working. The women cultivate the small fields, all the way from turning over the soil to the harvest, entirely by hand. Although the women are not veiled, they are extremely shy, and often upon sight of a stranger disappear in the bushes within seconds. When they have no opportunity to hide, they simply pull their large head kerchief over their faces and turn their backs to the stranger.

They normally wear a dress of red and black decorated with silver-looking trinkets, a black scarf and moccasins. Each carries a conical basket about three-feet high and a wooden, pronged fork about their height. The latter seems to be used as a pitchfork. The dress of the Wai women is a bit more distinctive than the other women encountered. They wear their hair long, sometimes in long braids. Their dress is black but has a wide white sash around the waist. On their legs they have tightly bound a kind of red legging or pantaloon. On their backs they wear the skin of a small animal, part of which seems to come around under the neck. The skin is apparently to protect their backs from the weight of the conical basket.

RELIGION

Each village has its mullah. His position is unique today in Nuristan, for he seems to be the one concrete link between the central authority, which is equated with Islam, and the village. As the watchdog over the religion of the people, he serves, in effect, as the guardian of everything that Kabul stands for. His role is not an easy one, for, although the old pagan gods and rituals are not actively worshipped, the people still seem to cling to many of the symbols – i.e. dances, songs and festive days – of the old religion. Although dying out, the stories of the old gods and legends are still known among the older men and held in respect. Paganism in all its manifestations is not yet stamped out. In scores of ways when travelling through the rest of Afghanistan one sees evidences of devotion to Islam, but among the Sefid Posh we saw not one indication to suggest that Islam is a practised religion of the people. In fact, in several villages up the Pech we detected a sharp cleavage between the maleks and the mullahs. We could only surmise that the unwillingness of the mullahs to be among those to greet us as we came into the village indicated their hostility. In Wama, in fact, the malek told us that the mullah had refused to see us, and it was this knowledge of the mullah's attitude towards us that prevented the maleks of Wama from holding dances for us that night. Only in Pashki did we meet the mullah, and only after the strong-willed malek had sent for him to escort us through the mosque.

We saw no effigies, but this is probably not surprising in view of the fact that they were almost all removed when the area was converted to Islam. Although we saw no cemeteries we did run across, near Waigel village, several isolated graves, which stood about four feet above the ground. The sides were made of wood and had intricate carvings all over them.

ADMINISTRATION

The link between the central government in Kabul and the Nuristanis of the Pech and Waigel is very tenuous. The authorities immediately responsible for the area, the Hakem and the Aliqadar, had never been into the region, although the latter's chief clerk had made some 12 trips. The government does conscript for the army. The Waigel Valley, for example, has a quota of 100 men every two years. No figures were available for the Pech Valley, but it was our impression that the number was considerably less than for the Waigel. As noted above, the mullah in the village, the guardian of the faith, is perhaps the individual closest to Kabul. Dealing with a comparatively recently converted people, he is extremely jealous of any incursions against Islamic institutions or the power that supports them. Apart from this the Sefid Posh, and the rest of the Nuristanis, are left unmolested by the central government. As a whole the Sefid Posh do not seem to be harried by Kabul, nor does there seem to be any resentment against the government. If anything, if the government continues not to molest them, it may well count on them for support in time of any emergency. The Wamaites supported Kabul against the Safis during their revolt in 1945/1946 and there is no indication that their sentiments have changed. The Safis have never forgiven the Wamaites for this action. The Wais take pride in the fact that their men have distinguished themselves in the service of the throne and supply many of the bodyguards for the royal palace.

CONTACT WITH THE OUTSIDE WORLD

The Sefid Posh have probably had as little contact with foreigners as the people of any region in Afghanistan. This contact has been limited to a few journalists and scientific expeditions into the area, which at most have spent several days in any given village. Neither the ideological war between East and West nor the economic development programmes supported by either side have had an impact on the area. The people realise that the Pakistani border is not too distant, that some of their supplies, such as axes and eye lotion, come from there and that some of their kindred live across the line, but they seem to have no special feeling of friendship or hostility towards the Pakistanis. The British they regard as clever but, here again, seem neither drawn to them nor repelled. The Germans are known favourably by their several expeditions into the region. They are curious about the Russians and have heard vaguely that they are godless. This they have never fully accepted, but when told that it was true they were visibly impressed. They have heard of America but know nothing about it. (I took the occasion to distribute judiciously among the literate maleks along the trip some 20 copies of a coloured and illustrated brochure in the Farsi language on President Eisenhower's recent visit to Kabul. The brochure was something of a sensation among all who saw it, and was enthusiastically received, with requests for additional copies if they could be spared. Since we were carrying all our supplies on our backs, the number of copies of printed material necessarily had to be limited.)

MORE DETAILS ON DIFFERENT GROUPS

Wama

The village of Wama, also called Tsaru, literally hangs on the side of a steep mountainside about 1400 feet above the Pech river. There is no easy access to it. The angle of the mountainside is about 65–70 degrees. The trail leading from the river virtually goes straight up the side of the cliff and is broken only by three rest platforms. It takes about an hour and 15 minutes to two hours to make the climb. The village is actually only about halfway up the mountainside, and is therefore subject to rockslides or avalanches from above. Quite recently a slide had killed a dozen people.

The 300 houses of Wama are divided into three districts, each self-governing. There are, therefore, three maleks, three mullahs and three mosques. A number of springs and small streams provide their water supply. The inhabitants have made the best use of their water by diverting the streams through to central locations for drinking and cleaning purposes. By the same technique, they have bathhouses with a steady and heavy stream of water for the shower. They had a cleaner and neater appearance than any of the other peoples encountered on the trip.

The houses of Wama are constructed generally like those of the other villages of the Sefid Posh. Because the village clutches itself to such a sheer cliff, access to the houses is more difficult, and unique, in Wama. Sometimes one of the houses is detached from the other houses. In this case the approach is by a log with hewn steps, by climbing up the protruding logs along the side of the house, or by simply stretching across the yard or so of space separating the houses. The houses take advantage of the terrain of the hillside as much as possible, but the front parts of some houses are on long poles or stilts slanted back into the cliff. The result is that the front porch sometimes has a drop of several hundred feet to the ground.

The position of malek is attained by the vote of the inhabitants of the village. The malek of the section of Wama where we stayed came from a family who had held the position for generations. Although the villagers select a leader from one family, they do not necessarily select the eldest son. The malek had two wives but was the exception, since most villagers had only one.

Although the malek was not old enough to remember the actual campaigns against Amir Abdur Rahman, he grew up in an atmosphere of a recently defeated people who had been forced to change their religion. He carried forth an intimate knowledge from his childhood of the old gods and rituals, even though officially the region had been by that time converted to Islam.

The Presuns

The Presuns are acknowledged to be of a different racial stock from any others in Nuristan. They occupy the upper Pech Valley and have grazing lands, which stretch, at least in one area, to the Waigel.

The area inhabited by the Presuns is high Alpine in nature, abounding in large pines and thick green grasses. The rocks, crags and steep canyon walls of the lower Pech have given way to the broader valleys, which permit both agriculture and cattle grazing. It is high enough that it is cool throughout the day in July, and clouds and mist often envelop the valley. All the surrounding mountains are snow-capped, and large ice fields come down to meet the Pech. Small irrigation ditches cover the fields, but they hardly seem necessary since there are so many rivulets coming down from the mountainsides. The lands are neatly terraced, usually marked off with rock hedges.

Pashki, the southernmost of the six villages, is located about 400 feet up the side of the hill on the edge of the wide valley, and in no way equals the formidable Wama. Two towers dominate the village: one is the guard tower, the other a combination minaret and storehouse. The buildings along the lower portion of the village are actually cattle sheds and fodder storage. The houses are located on the upper edge.

Despite their more favourable location from an agricultural and livestock standpoint in comparison with the Wamaites and Wais, the Presuns seem infinitely poorer and more emaciated. They appear dirtier and do not seem to have as good clothes as either the Wamaites or Wais, and their houses are not so well built or attractive. Even their diet is scantier. It is possible, however, that this poverty is the result of their almost complete isolation from the outside world. The little trade they carry on is in cattle, which they move over the high passes during the summer months in Badakhshan or in the direction of Kamdesh. The trade is usually for salt, tea and sugar.

While the houses of the Presuns resemble those of the Waigel or Wama, they are not so spacious; in fact, they barely permitted us to stand upright. Nor are they so well built, more rocks and clay being employed. There is nothing distinctive about their furniture and cooking utensils to set them apart from the other tribes of the Sefid Posh.

According to Robertson, the Presuns had a reputation in his day for being niggardly and selfish. This does not seem to hold true today, for despite their poverty they have a reputation for hospitality throughout the valley and even among the Safis. This stems largely from the fact that, at least in Pashki, there is a community warehouse. Each household contributes to a fund, which is used to feed travellers. No payment is accepted from the traveller.

The mosque in Pashki, the only one we succeeded in seeing the inside of, had two large rooms. One was where the Koran is read during the wintertime. It is about 25 feet square and has two small windows, which admit the light. The roof is supported by four massive but intricately carved columns placed in a ten foot square around the fire pit. The other room is about 25 by 50 feet. Down the centre are large beams across the ceiling, supported again by massive columns. Some of their most elaborate wood carved patterns are found in the mosque.

The malek of Pashki has held the position for 40 years, having inherited it from his father. The assistant malek was elected to his job 20 years ago. The position of malek does not carry with it any wealth. The malek of Pashki, for example, has 11 cows, whereas the assistant has 20 cows and about 300 head of sheep.

Waigel

The Wais occupy an area from near the conflux of the Waigel and Pech rivers at Ningrelam northwards about two-thirds up the Waigel. About halfway up the Waigel is located Waigel village, which is actually the twin villages of Qarie Waigel Olia and Qarie Waigel Sufla, the largest settlement. The area to the north, as far as the Gujer grazing lands and in places stretching across the mountains to the Pech, is used for pasture and agriculture. There are about 600 to 700 Wai houses in the valley.

The valley as a whole is very narrow, but there are a few flat areas along the river, which are used for intensive cultivation. The river is probably swifter than the Pech and drops much faster, sometimes falling 20 feet in a cataract. There are numerous bridges across the Waigel river.

Evidence of the industriousness of the Wais is apparent at every turn. Despite the rugged terrain of their valley they have utilised to good advantage every stretch of level land for growing corn and wheat. Additionally, they have large groves of walnut and mulberry trees and a few small vineyards. The northernmost reaches of their lands along the Waigel are used for Bandars, which are in sharp contrast to the crude shelters of the Presuns. The Wais live in the upper valley during the summer months but fall back to Waigel village for the winter. In the Bandars they have permanent cattle barns, which resemble some of the cattle huts located in Bavaria and the Tyrol, and are quite unlike anything else in Afghanistan. The first floor of the building, which is used for cattle, is made of logs, with very little wattle being used. Above this floor is a high, steeply slanted roof, the sides of which are open. During the winter this open attic is used for fodder storage but during the summer it serves as a comfortable living space. Corn and millet are grown in small terraced patches irrigated by run-off streams from the river. These cultivated plots stretch for a distance of some two hours' walk to the north and about an hour's walk below the village. Although the women seem to do most of the work, the older children are also pressed into service.

Waigel village is located at the conflux of three rivers, the Agok and Asma emptying into the Waigel. The Agok Valley leads to Kamdesh. One part of the village is located several hundred feet above the river, but the upper village is perched high on the mountain slope, perhaps 1000 feet above the valley floor. The houses of the village are well built and kept, and often have a wooden door with carved designs. The entire region is most picturesque and has a prosperous air about it. Despite the fact that it is about 12 hours' walk from the closest auto road over a difficult trail it gives the appearance of being in touch with civilisation. There are even a few houses with glass panes in the windows. The villagers seemed to have a plentiful supply of salt, sugar, tea and rice. The village has a school. The dress of the villagers is as much Afghan as it is Nuristani. Many of the elders wore medals presented to them by the Afghan government. The Wais have established a reputation since the days of Abdur Rahman for their bravery and loyalty to the central government at Kabul. They provide many of the bodyguards for the royal palace. One young man, the brother of the malek of the upper Waigel village, had recently returned to the village following the death of Shah Mahmud (the King's uncle and former Prime Minister), for whom he had served as personal bodyguard.

The upper and lower villages are both headed by maleks. Above these two men stands the Wakil. He is the son of a Hakem, and some ten years ago served as the representative from the Waigel Valley to the National Assembly in Kabul. He seemed to function as the chief of the Wais, since he had authority to hear and settle all cases in the Waigel. Some of the more serious ones he felt compelled to pass on to the Hakem in Manugai.

3 Reflections

A FASCINATING FIRST POST

(Nicholas Barrington)

After Persian language study in London and Iran, Kabul was my first post, and, for a diplomat, this usually presages a lasting interest in that place. I had a tiny house in the British embassy compound but it was my own, with a gentle Goanese cook. It was freezing in the winter, when scorpions used to come inside out of the cold. The community in Kabul was quite small and I began to know almost everybody, helped by being able to communicate in Persian, the lingua franca. More than most diplomats I had a wide range of Afghan friends, who were very hospitable.

I soon discovered that most of them were in some way related to the Afghan royal family, so I got hold of, and studied, a copy of their extended family tree. Several had married outside the ruling Durrani tribe; the best performer, going back a generation, was the Amir Habibullah, who had children by some 40 wives or consorts, of whom ten were from Nuristan. According to all the books this was a fascinating part of the country, rarely visited. One of the Amir's Nuristani consorts was the mother of the wife of Shah Mahmud Khan, the King's uncle and former Prime Minister, whose large family, like the old man himself, were charming and intelligent. They were one-quarter Nuristani. I played tennis with two of the younger sons.

Amir Abdur Rahman, who had united Afghanistan at the end of the nineteenth century, did this by dynastic marriages with prominent families, as well as by force. His armies had conquered Nuristan, formerly Kafiristan, and converted the people to Islam. Some of his son's liaisons may have been diplomatic. But the Nuristanis also had the reputation of being handsome and beautiful, many of them being fair-haired with fair complexions. Some prisoners were brought as slaves and attendants at court, and subsequently advanced by merit to high positions, including at least one general.

All this was part of Afghanistan's rich history, in which I took great interest. It was stimulated by a visit by the famous British historian Arnold Toynbee, who took me with him to visit ancient sites, running ahead of his escorts in his enthusiasm, and who gave an impressive lecture in Kabul on 'Afghanistan: Crossroads of History'. We could travel much of the country perfectly securely in those days. It became a route for enterprising students driving overland to India. Since the Foreign Office in London was little interested in this remote place we took opportunities to travel, and the most adventurous trip that I made, or have ever made, was to Nuristan.

It was great to be fortified by the companionship of two other diplomatic friends and colleagues. The three of us got on very well together, and each made a significant contribution to this expedition. Despite my best researches in the extensive embassy library there were no adequate maps and little useful information about Nuristan, so we really did not know what to expect there. Young at the time, I found the patches of hazardous terrain nothing but a challenge, though, thinking back, how absurd it was of me to travel in gym shoes! It was only in Wama that we felt menaced, and it was there that I had one of the most rewarding contacts – with the old man, described in the narrative, who had accompanied Amir Habibullah on his official visit to India. We 'clicked' immediately, as one can do with people across barriers of age, sex, race, religion and culture, and I was very touched when he gave me the stick, which I still proudly possess, and treasure. I also keep the dagger, illustrated in this book, that I bought at Waigel.

Although we got an overall impression of life in the two valleys of central Nuristan that we visited, places seen by very few before us, we only scratched the surface, of course, in knowing what these people really thought and how they lived. It was clear that they were suspicious of government, which left them very much to themselves, and that they had their own established system of choosing maleks as leaders. As with most remote communities, the people rarely travelled beyond their own village or area and knew little of the outside world. Hospitality towards travellers was ingrained, partly also so they could be tapped for information. Relationships with the local mullahs seemed obscure, and to vary. At a modest level the people were self-sufficient, stuck in a kind of time warp. Any economic development looked bound to come very slowly.

Back in Kabul the government was run with a firm hand by the King's cousin and brother-in-law, Sardar Daoud, who was taking cautious steps to modernise the country. The King was a passive constitutional figure, though we had the impression that the combined views of the close royal family – Nadir Shah's brothers and their children – had influence at weekly dinners in the palace. I was actually witness to the most dramatic act of liberalisation when, at a function in the National Stadium, the wife of the Foreign Minister (Daoud's brother) appeared in a head scarf, rather than under the completely covering burqa. All around me jaws dropped in astonishment. The next day her daughters, and then other ladies, appeared without veils, and this spread quickly to educated women. Some men were reported to have taken new young second wives so that their boasts about the beauty of their spouses should not be exposed!

Sardar Daoud's foreign policies were less progressive. Because of his promotion of the unrealistic Pashtunistan issue, which would have meant the dismemberment of Pakistan, relations with that country deteriorated. All Pakistanis were expelled. This involved security staff and drivers at the embassy, including the loyal Reza Khan whom I had taken to the Pech Valley. Rather than employ Afghans at that stage we imported Gurkhas for the embassy.

I got on more easily with other ambassadors in those days than with my own. Sir Michael Gillett was an eccentric figure of the old school, with monocle and piebald goatee beard, whose main interest was Chinese calligraphy. But it was to him that I owe my record of our trip to

Nuristan, because he made me sit down and write it all up while the memory of the trip was fresh.

When I left Afghanistan I took my photographs and the account of the journey with me round the world. From 1965 to 1967, when I was back in the area, as first secretary in Pakistan's then interim capital, Rawalpindi, I visited Kabul several times on vacation. Daoud had resigned in 1963 and the King was in charge. A young lawyer and good friend whom I had seen a lot of in Kabul, Musa Shafiq, was advisor to the King and told me that many of the ideas we had discussed together had been incorporated into the new constitution he had helped draft. He told me that Daoud had resigned out of pique because he had wanted to become President. Shafiq, who bridged two worlds as the son of a respected Islamic scholar who had studied both at Al Azhar in Cairo and in America, later became Foreign Minister and Prime Minister. He was sidelined when Daoud took his revenge on the King and declared himself President, with leftist military support, in 1973. When the Communists slaughtered Daoud and his family in a bloody coup in 1978 Shafiq also disappeared, as did my tennis-playing friends, sons of Shah Mahmud. I was serving in Cairo at that time.

These sad events had their repercussions in all parts of the country, even in Nuristan. In the intervening years two British visitors had recorded journeys to 'our' valleys. John Heath, head of chancery in the British embassy, visited the Pech Valley in 1963. He went up to Safrigal, 'a dirty and unsavoury place' perched on a high rock, which we had avoided in the lower valley. At Doab his party turned left up the Kantiwar Valley to the village itself, where he was told he was only the fourth foreigner to visit in 25 years, and then crossed beyond Wama to reach the Parun Valley near Pashki. He went on to Ishtiwe before coming back down the Pech-Parun Valley. In 1969 Christopher Rundle from the embassy went up the Pech Valley and across from Ishtiwe to Kamdesh. He was accompanying Peter Levi, poet and Jesuit priest, who recorded the trip in his book *The Light Garden of the Angel King* (see 'Bibliography' annex). The writer Bruce Chatwin was also in the party. The Oxford anthropologist Schuyler Jones, who had first visited Nuristan in 1960, carried out fieldwork in the Waigel Valley between 1965 and 1970.

Nothing had changed much in the early years following our visit, though areas of Nuristan were becoming increasingly Islamicised. The situation was different, however, when groups of Mujahideen began to organise themselves to fight the Communists, with the help of arms from Pakistan, paid for by the Americans. One of the most effective leaders was Ahmed Shah Masud, operating in the Panjshir Valley and farther north. The main route for taking arms to him, and for journalists to visit him, was through the upper reaches of Nuristan. A major route is shown in the map in Sandy Gall's book *Behind Russian Lines*. It started from Chitral in Pakistan, where visitors had to pay fees to a mini, self-proclaimed independent state called 'Doulat' that functioned for ten years, led by a radical mullah. It then came down to Pol-i-Rustom, north of Kamdesh, and then across to the top of the Parun Valley, down and across to Kantiwar, and then north-west to the upper Panjshir. There were five major passes in all, usable for pack animals with heavy loads. This passage of men and arms inevitably affected the lives of all people in the area. They became armed themselves and had more money. New local strongmen emerged, some linked with different Mujahideen parties. The area was important enough for the Communist regimes, the Mujahideen and, later, the Taliban to seek to increase their influence there. People in the villages got caught up in these events and became less insular.

I was aware of all this when I was posted as ambassador to Pakistan for six years in 1987 at the height of the Mujahideen struggle against the Russians. I had contact with all the principal Mujahideen leaders in Peshawar. Nuristan was, however, a sideshow to the main events: the departure of the Russians, the fragmentation of the Soviet empire in Central Asia and the internecine battles between Mujahideen groups.

The closest I came to Nuristan in those days was to visit the Kalash people in Chitral, relatives of Nuristanis divided from them by the international frontier and mountain ranges, living in three small valleys where many of them maintain their ancient religion and traditions. Maureen Lines, an Englishwomen who has lived among the Kalash and speaks their language, became a friend. She made me very conscious of the damage done by deforestation not only in Chitral but also over the border in Nuristan.

My old friend Max Klimburg in Vienna is probably the best expert today on Nuristan, which he visited several times between 1971 and 1976, and again between 1987 and the present day. He knows the Pech-Parun and Waigel Valleys well. It remains to be seen how much recent turbulent events have permanently disturbed the malek structure and the culture and beliefs of the Nuristani people. It is sad that the more extreme form of Islam seems to have found a footing there. It is to be hoped that peace and law and order will return to all of Afghanistan after the defeat of the Taliban, and that the Nuristanis will be able to maintain a considerable degree of local autonomy while accepting development (various agencies are working there already), including education, better health, electricity, etc. Roads, or at least jeep tracks, are important, of course, for development, but they also allow incursion from outside. Perhaps one day there will be tourist hotels in Nuristan, as there are among their neighbours the Kalash. Hopefully, these will benefit the Nuristanis themselves and include cultural events that will show that they have not forgotten their ancient traditions.

Sadly, as this book was going to print, the situation in Afghanistan was becoming increasingly infected by the disastrous events in Iraq. The ill-planned and illegal (in UN terms) invasion of Iraq by US and coalition forces increased support for Al Qaeda-type extremists round the world, as some of us had warned. London and Madrid suffered. Karzai's task in Kabul was made more difficult. Remote Nuristan was not immune. In a high-profile incident in July 2005 an American Special Forces helicopter trying to rescue servicemen on the ground was shot down by missile, killing all 16 men on board – America's greatest casualty toll in Afghanistan so far. The press reported that this took place in the Waigel Valley, which had seemed so peaceful years before.

WALKING BACK INTO THE STONE AGE

(Reinhard Schlagintweit)

In the spring of 1958 I started my period of service at the German embassy in Kabul. In the beginning I lived in a hotel, the only one at that time that was suitable for foreigners. To make my way to the office in the morning I climbed into one of the open cabs that waited in front of the hotel. The coachman cracked his whip, and the little lean horse trotted through the newly paved avenues to the new part of the town, where the better-off people lived.

It was to this part of town that we later moved. We took one of the few houses that had a sheet metal roof. The kitchen and the servant quarters were, like most other houses in the city, still covered with clay. When it rained the cook spread a cloth over the hearth, in order that the raindrops would not get into the soup. In the autumn we bought fuel for the winter. Coal dust from remote valleys in the north of the country was unloaded in front of the house. Day labourers used to sit in the yard and mix the dust with clay and water to form briquettes for our stoves.

During embassy garden parties, we often talked about the influence of the Soviet Union or discussed the obscure distribution of power within the Afghan royal family. I also remember the Deputy Foreign Minister telling me about the spell of religious bliss he had experienced sitting at the tomb of a Sufi poet while he was ambassador at Delhi, and the chief of protocol quoting poems by Rumi and Hafiz. Many of my friends were mystics, and those who spoke German used words such as 'tenderness' or 'love of God'.

At that time there was no other Muslim country where religious rules were so rigorously observed. Even the wives of both the King and his cousin, the Prime Minister, wore the burqa, the whole-body veil, when they left the palace in their Bentleys.

I imagined that life in the capital cities of German regional states, some 250 years ago, in many respects must have resembled that in Kabul in 1960, and their patriarchal and authoritarian rule would have been similar.

Each trip into the country led us even deeper into the past. The quaint, poor villages tucked down at the edge of torrential mountain rivers lacked electricity, schools and doctors. All buildings were built of clay, the menacing fort-like mansions sitting between the fields, and the huge walls of Ghazni towering over the most beautiful camel market in the country. If we stopped on the road, often we were invited to a wedding. This was usually celebrated by the whole village in the shade of large, magnificent trees, with drums and wind instruments and mountains of steaming rice. Everywhere we encountered testimonials to much earlier times, like the Buddhas of Bamian, or the huge ruins at the lower end of the Helmand Valley.

Our hike through Nuristan was a very special trip into the past. Here we encountered not ruins from an historical past but life in a pre-historic epoch. Many villages that we entered had never seen a machine. There existed no vehicles, no wheels, no police, and no radios. No axe or saw had even disturbed the virgin, light-filled forests through which we walked as through bright cathedrals. No human foot had left its track. Until a few decades before, an archaic religion using wooden idols and sorcery had survived in the valleys, protected by snow-clad mountains and huge rock barriers. The melancholy sounds of a one-stringed instrument, which an old man once played for us by the light of a torch, made us sense their mourning over the loss of their gods' protective and nourishing power.

One day we pitched our tent beside a Bandar, a mountain encampment, at an altitude of some 10,000 feet. We had crossed a 15,000-foot pass, covered by soft deep snow, and, exhausted, were grateful for the friendly hospitality of the small group of men who, together with numerous children, tended their sheep and goats.

In need of an even surface for the tent, we had to dig into the hillside. A young shepherd helped us. In order to scrape the earth and move the stones, he used a handy, sharp rock. Suddenly I realised: 'we are in the Stone Age!' There was no spade, no shovel; the shepherd's only tool was a stone. Even the pots and pans that the herdsmen used, both for making butter, and in the evening, to drum out the wild rhythms to which they sang and danced, were made of wood. All the other objects, too, were home-made: their woollen clothes, the pieces of hide they used for shoes, and even the strap of leather that held the door in its frame.

The men told us that their people lived almost exclusively off products that they had produced themselves: corn bread, walnuts, cheese, meat, honey. An axe and a couple of knives were the only metal objects they possessed. Such imported items, as well as salt and sugar, were purchased with the proceeds from the sale of butter, which the men carried into the valleys on marches that lasted several days.

That evening we lived in an archaic world. We witnessed the unbroken – it seemed to us – strength of the shepherds and sensed their mysterious strangeness. Under a gigantic yew tree in front of our encampment huge pieces of wood were burning. The shepherds sang and danced. Farther away, fascinated, enigmatically beautiful children observed them in silence. The oldest shepherd, with rhythmic movements and erotic songs, worked himself up into a bewildering frenzy. Finally, his sons led him away to recover from the trance. The fire died down, and the ecstasy of the night faded.

* * *

Sometimes we are inclined to idealise distant periods of human development and to believe their seemingly genuine lifestyle to be preferable to our over-civilised way of life. We forget, however, that in those times people were helplessly exposed to want and disease, and lived under the scourge of local wars, robbery and serfdom. In a secluded region such as Nuristan all this was true until only a few years ago. We became aware of this lack of security when the shepherds implored the policemen, whom the Afghan Minister of the Interior had attached to us, to help them bring back the animals that armed nomads had stolen a couple of days ago. The police, like the robbers, had firearms. The Nuristanis did not.

It is one of the conceived achievements of civilisation to have created, in many regions of the world, through the combination of religious law and strong state power, an internal peace. Afghanistan, which for the first time evolved into a kind of state at the end of the nineteenth century, repeatedly tried to establish a durable order of this kind as a precondition for political and social development. Again and again the attempt failed and provoked a catastrophe. The centre was not strong enough to integrate the divergent views of the population regarding the roles of the state and of religion. Sometimes, however, it succeeded in creating relatively stable conditions, at least for the densely populated, fertile parts of the country. Our trip happened to fall within such a period.

Days later, when we returned to our cars and were heading for home, we came upon a spectacular scene of medieval order. Court-day was held in the village, the seat of the district administration. The central square was crowded with men. The judge, a young cleric, clad in flawless white garments, was seated under the roof of an open pavilion. On his lap sat his three-year-old little son, whose big eyes observed the procedures without disturbing the process of justice. Next to the judge was a table for the secular power. This was where the district chief sat, among the documents, with the court scribe at his side. It seemed to us, as passing observers, that the religious and secular authorities, as well as the ordinary subjects, were part of a functioning system and that this was a good state of affairs.

Of course, this archetypal picture concealed big shadows: poverty, the arbitrary exercise of power, oppression. Not much later, far deeper conflicts that had then not yet been visible ripped the country apart. The government failed to show a convincing route into modernity for a young generation that was becoming increasingly restless. Progressive groups of students, seduced by the neighbour to the north, the Soviet Union, considered socialism the right way to overcome the country's backwardness. Islamic students, too, demanded change and social justice, though not with the help of Marx but exclusively through the Koran.

We know the disastrous consequences of this failure. All the evil spirits of Afghanistan's past seemed to have returned: civil war, ethnic persecution, and the decay of the state, interference by powerful neighbours, destitution and mass displacement of the population.

These catastrophes have also touched and changed Nuristan. They carried, however, a lesser amount of devastation into its remote settlements than to the rest of the country. The forbidding physical nature of the valleys and mountains still grants a certain protection. During the war against the Soviet Union convoys of bearers carrying arms to the freedom fighters used to walk alongside the rivers. The villages moved nearer to the riverside. Later primitive tracks, passable by jeep, were dug where before one could only walk. For a few years the Taliban dominated the more important places. Some of their warriors might still be hiding in retreats like the Bandar we visited. The forests of Nuristan are now being recklessly exploited. But the big trucks carrying lumber into Pakistan seem to come rather from the wider Kunar Valley on the Pakistani frontier than from the virgin forests of the upper Waigel, which we had crossed.

Some valleys used to report to the Taliban regime, which confined its rule to indirect control. Most parts were loyal to the Northern Alliance. The weakness of the state allowed more political autonomy, but not more religious freedom. The increasing polarisation of Afghanistan by the Islamic and socialistic ideologies, which had already intervened before the beginning of the war against the Soviet Union, rather increased the power of local secular and religious leaders. But now the village clerics are no longer sent out from Kabul. They are Nuristanis who, lured by generous stipends, were trained at fundamentalist colleges in Pakistan. They insist that extreme religious rules be strictly observed. There is no more dancing and singing, and the women are seen even less in public than before. Thus the enforced Islamisation begun 100 years ago continues from within, although less bloodily.

Progress and modernity enter from a different door. Foreign non-governmental organisations arrived in Nuristan together with the freedom fighters. After the defeat of the Taliban they increased their efforts. To the more accessible villages, they are bringing electricity, health, education, economic improvement and an easier access to the markets in the plains.

Yet change will be very slow. Not only the mountains and gorges but the zeal of Nuristan's current religious leaders work as barriers against modernity. As a consequence Nuristan is being deprived of its cultural identity while remaining in poverty and isolation.

APPREHENSIONS OF A CYNIC

(J.T. Kendrick – 2002)

It is very painful to reflect on Kafiristan. Here is a people, society and culture, so old, probably thousands of years, unchanged in its mountain seclusion, on the verge of becoming 'civilised' with all the accoutrements of today's modern world. Some things the region urgently needs, such as health care and education, but for many other elements perhaps it would be better to let the area remain in its pristine state.

But, before examining the possible bleak future of this world of the past, there are a few personal impressions of these people and their culture that are satisfying to reflect on after 40 years. One was the hospitality and warmth of the people in welcoming us in what, for many, was their first sight of a foreigner. Their world had been sealed off from outside contact for hundreds of years. It was a time warp going back to the Stone Age. In contrast to the warmth of the people was the obviously cool and sometimes apparently hostile attitude of the mullahs, the guardians of Islam assigned to each village, who, by their absence, indicated that we were the incarnation of evil threatening their charges. At the same time, once out of range of the mullahs, particularly in the shepherds' Bandars (encampments) in the high mountains, the men expressed themselves fully by their dancing, their singing old and forbidden pagan songs and their longing for a past era. They had a unique spirit and love of life, which had survived for millennia.

Other deep impressions left of that visit were the impenetrability of the land: long stretches without even a trail, over which a pack animal could not survive or make its way; precipitous cliffs, with huts hanging precariously against the face of the mountain, often hundreds of feet, or perhaps a thousand, above the valley floor; and, finally there were the wild rivers swollen from the melting snows of the higher peaks, alongside which, with only thin embankments, we were forced to make our way for miles. Falling into those raging waters would have meant certain drowning.

There was the long, exhausting trek over the glacier, which shifted from a hard-pack in the morning to soft snow in the afternoon and where one sank to the hips with each arduous step. We eventually emerged into a high land of grazing sheep, with shepherds who tended both their animals and a herd of young children from the village below. The wives and mothers tilled the fields over the summer months while the fathers and children lived in protective shelters, which resembled caves.

The mood and actions of the people could be completely baffling. For example, the few men whom the elders had assigned to assist us as guides and porters to the next juncture were unpredictable in their relationship with each other. They would be vigorously quarrelling one minute, and the next break out into song and dance.

On a personal note, there were my own unsuccessful efforts to catch a photo of a Nuristani woman's unveiled face. Nicholas was angry about my pursuit of the photos, as a violation of local religion and customs and the hospitality granted to us. The women were reputed to be among the most beautiful in the world. Over the years they had been prizes of the Islamic world, particularly those women living in the border regions of Nuristan/Kafiristan. They were subject to being kidnapped and then sold, or confined in a marriage to an Afghan as one of several wives to which he might be entitled.

Finally, I remember traversing a 100-foot-wide sheer cliff, some 50 feet above the wild river. We found ourselves edging across one set of cracks in the rock face searching for a toehold, while reaching for a similar set of cracks at arm's length over our heads. We were with several police officers attempting to make sideways movements along the cliff's trail, cursing the crazy foreigners for getting them into this predicament. Personally, I was enjoying myself, probably because I had scaled mountainous terrain in my youth. But the police were horrified. They completed the traverse with an obvious show of relief because it had been without incident or loss of life.

As regards the three uniformed police officers, with whom we eventually established a good relationship, my one regret at the end of the trek was in neglecting to be certain that the expenses for the replacement of their tattered uniforms and broken shoes would be assumed by their administration, and the costs not placed on them personally.

During the 40 years after we left Afghanistan there occurred rapid developments and increasingly deplorable conditions, which touched the entire area. In contrast to the stability that the regime had enjoyed during our stay, the country had fallen into its old practice of internecine fighting – which gave the Soviet Union the opening to endorse a Communist coup, followed by invasion. The resistance of the Afghan people led to the expulsion of the Soviets, but also to the rise of the Taliban from the seeds of the conflict.

The Taliban had no experience in the administration of government, nor concern for the needs of the population. They concentrated on imposing a religious state with a narrow interpretation of Islam and Shari'a law. Having travelled among the Hazaras (adherents of the Shia branch of Islam) I was particularly concerned about the victimisation of that minority. Hazara women were abducted and made the sexual slaves of men victorious in battle. For most of their time in power the Taliban relied on heroin production and export to the West as an important source of revenue.

The most distressing attribute of the Taliban regime was its readiness to support a terrorist threat against the Western world. The Muslim radicals who had joined the struggle against the Communists became the recruits for the Al-Qaeda network, protected by the Taliban. Their chief, Osama bin Laden, was particularly bitter against the United States for basing American troops in Saudi Arabia, and invading Iraq. He is purported to have issued a 'fatwa', a religious ruling, to all Muslims to kill Americans and to 'liberate' the entire Middle East (although he had no authority to do so). He and his associates were responsible for a series of atrocities against Americans, culminating in the attack on the World Trade Center on 11 September 2001. The Taliban persistently refused to give up or expel Osama bin Laden.

This growth of terrorism did not happen overnight. The policy of the United States regarding Afghanistan from about 1985 was, in my view, ill-advised. The difficulties stem from a conservative, essentially isolationist Congress, with certain leaders having limited background in foreign affairs, coming to the fore in congressional committees and attempting to play politics, in order to restrict the administration's foreign policy and set its own agenda. As a result, money for international assistance and other aspects of foreign affairs was drastically scaled back, so that expertise in many areas, especially in Central Asia, was lost. In particular, the Department of State fell victim. Its programmes were cut to the bone, posts were closed, management depleted, communications and computer equipment became obsolete, and the majority of missions overseas were deprived of established security measures. The CIA also suffered a loss of knowledgeable operatives. Some of the cuts may have been justified but most represented a petty vendetta.

The US focus on the Cold War resulted in the abandonment of Central Asia, including Afghanistan. This situation allowed the birth of a worldwide terrorist movement.

Today the framework of a new government is in place for Afghanistan, and there is an agenda for progress to a more permanent structure. But probably no country faces such formidable tasks: more than 1 million people addicted to opium; more than 1.5 million children underfed and many orphaned; a large percentage of the population, particularly women, undereducated and illiterate; animosities among the various tribal ethnic groups, interference in internal affairs by hostile neighbouring countries; economic hardship through prolonged drought and destroyed industry; progress limited by religious extremists; and a large refugee population that has fled because of war, religious oppression and economic poverty. It is truly a wrecked state.

In my view, relations between Islam and the Western world are also at a precarious stage, and now need sensitive handling. To add to the internal difficulties, the situation in Afghanistan has intensified Muslim hatred of the Western world. The West must make clear to the Muslim world that there is respect for Islam, although not acceptance of the actions of an extremist minority. The United States, for its part, cannot afford to take unilateral political actions that will inflame the Muslim world even further and lend credibility to the terrorists.

As for Nuristan itself, I am fearful that the age-old culture and way of life of these people is in danger of being snuffed out. I do not believe that the new religion imposed on them is fully accepted, even after 100 years. Perhaps I have become a cynic in my old age. I accept that the area is in dire need of modern improvements, such as better health care and education. However, these changes should clearly be the choice of the people, not imposed upon them. I would hate to see the trappings of 'progress' imposed on these ancient people. It is my hope that they be left as they have been – to grow their grapes, make their wine, worship as they wish. Hidden in their impenetrable valleys, the Nuristani may be illiterate or poor by our standards, but they have maintained a fruitful existence with an indomitable spirit of life. I wish we could have left them in their former state, for I think we have much to learn from them. But, alas, I fear it is not to be.

Annex 1: Summary History of Afghanistan – Long and Turbulent

Although Afghanistan as a separate state came into existence only in 1747, the land of Afghanistan has a history going back thousands of years. One of the first cities in Central Asia was Balkh, the vast ruins of which lie not far from Mazar-i-Sharif in northern Afghanistan. Since ancient times it was known as 'the Mother of Cities', probably because, apart from early civilisations in the river valleys of the Nile, Euphrates, Indus and Yellow River, urban centres were rare. In the millennia before Christ most of northern Europe and Asia was occupied by nomadic people loosely called Scythians, who had no cities. Balkh was the birthplace of Zoroaster, prophet of the first of the great world religions, who lived in the area around 800 BC (scholars are divided on his dates).

Balkh would already have been the centre of transport routes in those days: north and south to India, and particularly east and west, the forerunner of the silk route to China. The historian Arnold Toynbee called Afghanistan 'the Crossroads of History'. Among the items transported, right from the earliest days, was lapis lazuli, from mines that are still worked near Munjan in a remote corner of north-eastern Afghanistan by the mouth of the Wakhan Corridor. All the brilliant dark blue lapis in Egyptian and other ancient tombs came from there.

The Indo-European peoples who came down into India, Iran and Europe from the north around 1000 BC, speaking related languages if not being of similar race, eventually settled as farmers in Central Asia and Afghanistan, as well as further south. They formed part of the world's first great empire, that of the Persians, which spread at its height as far as the Indus and Oxus rivers in around 500 BC. That empire was conquered in 330 BC by Alexander the Great of Macedon, who chased the last Achemenaean Emperor to the borders of modern Afghanistan near Herat, and finally overcame him and his successor, the governor of

Bactria (the Afghan plain between the Oxus and Hindu Kush). Thereafter, Alexander spent several years of his short life subduing the peoples north of the Oxus. His name is still remembered in the remotest valleys. He founded cities on the sites of modern Herat, Kandahar and Bagram, north of Kabul. The foundations of a classic Greek city were also discovered at Ai Khanom, north-east of Kunduz near the Oxus.

Alexander eventually crossed into India north of the Khyber Pass, not far from modern Nuristan, where some claim that a few of his soldiers may have settled. They certainly settled in the cities that he founded, and when Alexander died in Babylon on his way home to Greece, and his empire was divided among his generals, these Greeks became part of the successor Seleucid Empire. On their eastern borders the Seleucids had to combat a new power growing up in northern India, which was to unite most of the subcontinent in a way that did not happen again until the Moghuls and the British. This was the Mauryan Empire, founded by Chandragupta. His grandson Asoka converted to Buddhism and ruled wisely around 250 BC, including over south-eastern Afghanistan. When the Mauryan Empire collapsed the local Greeks survived, forming their own Greek-Bactrian kingdoms. By this time they were cut off from Greece by the rising power of the Parthians in Iran.

After an eruption of Scythians (Sakas) from the north around 100 BC a new power came on the scene: the Yueh-Chih, or Kushans, had been pushed to the west and south by Huns and other nomadic movements. They came down into Afghanistan and then northern India, patronising Buddhism and maintaining aspects of Greek culture. Their hybrid Greek–Asian culture is known as Gandhara. Prominent sites include Hadda, near Jalalabad, but Buddhism never seems to have penetrated the remote valleys of Nuristan, where the people continued to practice an early form of polytheistic Hinduism. The most prominent Kushan king, Kanishka, ruled in about AD 200, and it was after this period (although authorities now say it may have been up to 400 years later) that the massive statutes of Buddha were carved into the wall of rock at Bamian, in central Afghanistan – now, sadly, destroyed by the Taliban. The new Persian Sassanian Empire had by now replaced the Parthians. In the third century AD the Sassanians defeated the Kushans, but 200 years later their eastern territories were lost to an avalanche of White Huns

(Ephthalites), the rearguard of the Hun hordes sweeping across northern Asia and into Europe. These went on to destroy the Hindu Gupta Empire in India, and their modern descendants are probably the Rajputs.

Exhausted by fighting against Rome, the Sassanian Persian Empire was finally overthrown by the Arabs, bringing the new religion of Islam with great energy and fervour into north Africa, the Middle East and as far as Central Asia. The conquered territories would henceforth owe allegiance to the Caliphates in Damascus, and then Baghdad, but outlying areas enjoyed considerable autonomy. For a time Hindu kingdoms from the south (the Hindu-shahis) controlled the Kabul area. The Soghdian Empire in Transoxiana (the lands north of the river), defeated by the Arabs after some resistance, gave way to the Islamic Samanid Empire in the same area. This, in turn, was eventually overwhelmed by groups of Turkish nomads, following after the Huns. Most became early converts to Islam. The first great Turkish kingdom, that of the Ghaznavids, was named after their main capital at Ghazni in Afghanistan, which was a centre of scholarship as well as a military power. Mahmud of Ghazni's armies raided far into Sindh and the Punjab around 1000 AD, beginning a process of Muslim invasions of India that was to continue long afterwards. Other Turkish dynasties subsequently ruled in Delhi and dominated the area, except for a period when the Ghorid dynasty, who were probably Tajiks, succeeded the Ghaznavids and ruled from their own Afghan capital at Ghor, site of the long-lost (but now rediscovered) Minaret of Djam. The Seljuk Turks in Iran made puppets of the last Abbasid Caliphs. The world was now ready for the cataclysmic Mongol invasions of the thirteenth century, and there were many Turks in the Mongol armies. Genghis Khan himself chased his last major opponent in Central Asia, the Khwarazm-Shah, whose capital had been at Urganj, near Khiva, through Afghanistan to the Indus river.

The Mongols demolished cities that resisted them and struck terror everywhere. They were originally open to all religions, but the local branches of the family of Genghis Khan, the Il Khanids in greater Iran and the Chagatai nomads in Central Asia, eventually accepted Islam. In 1270 Marco Polo travelled through Afghanistan on his way to the court of the Mongol Emperor in China, Kublai Khan. The Hazara people of the high Hindu Kush in central Afghanistan have Mongol ancestry and may well be the remnants of Mongol armies of that time, though there are theories that they arrived in a group at a somewhat later date. In contrast to the vast majority of the Afghan population the Hazaras became Shias.

It was not long before another larger-than-life man emerged with dreams of world conquest. Tamerlaine ('Timur the Lame'), of Chagatai Turkish stock, went further than the Mongols and conquered Delhi, as well as large areas of Asia and the Middle East, also leaving a trail of destruction and massacres behind him, though he was a patron of the arts in his capital of Samarkand. He was one of the few powerful commanders who were recorded as striking at the inhabitants of Nuristan, who were forced to retreat into their impenetrable mountains. But, to his frustration, he did not conquer them; they continued to resist conversion to Islam. Tamerlaine took Delhi in 1400. He died on a journey to attack China.

One hundred years later a more admirable man, with both Timurid and Mongol blood, came on the scene. Having been forced out of his inheritance in Central Asia by more invading Turks, Babur established himself in the Kabul area. Like most people in those days he travelled round the western end of the Hindu Kush, via Herat. He noted in his fascinating memoirs all he saw, including the sophisticated life of the later Timurid rulers in Herat, where fine painting and music flourished, surrounded by exquisitely tiled buildings (of which a few remain). Established at last in Kabul, he used it as a base for conquering India, where he founded the Moghul dynasty that ruled for over 200 years. But he never lost his affection for Kabul, where he is buried, in a great terraced garden, heavily damaged in recent years by neglect and fighting. There were no fine buildings in Kabul, however, to match the incomparable palaces and tombs, such as the Taj Mahal, which the Moghuls constructed in India.

This was the period of the three magnificent Islamic land empires that held sway before sea power shifted the world balance of power to Europe. The Ottoman Empire spread round the shores of the Mediterranean in the west; in Iran, the Safavid monarchs, Shias, from their beautiful capital at Isfahan, fought with the Moghuls for Kandahar and dominated Herat. As so often in its history, Afghanistan was the subject of a three-way power struggle as the last of the major Turkic nomadic people, the Uzbeks, pressed from the north to seek fertile land. The Uzbeks crossed the

Oxus and settled in the Bactrian plains. The exciting traditional Afghan sport of Buzkeshi, with unfettered horsemen, harks back to those days of nomadic warriors. It is interesting that, having been passive and subdued for a couple of centuries under the Afghan state, the convulsions of the last 20 years seem to have revived some element of the Uzbeks' aggressive and violent character.

The Pushtun people of Afghanistan were, up to this point, mainly known for harassing passing armies. They were grouped into tribes of indeterminate, probably Indo-European, origin, speaking Pushtu, a language related to Persian (which remained the commercial and administrative lingua franca of the area). In 1720 they hit world headlines for the first time when Ghilzai tribesmen overthrew the Persian governor of Kandahar, went on to attack the enfeebled Safavid dynasty and, probably to their own surprise, took Isfahan. They were rough soldiers, who created havoc. The man who finally ousted them was the last of the great army conquerors in Asia: Nadir Shah, a Persian of Afshar Turkoman origin. He won victories against the Turks and in Central Asia, and, in 1738, came through Afghan territory to conquer Delhi, from where he took the Peacock Throne and the Koh-i-Noor diamond as booty. But on manoeuvres nine years later he was assassinated. The commander of his bodyguard, Ahmad Shah, was an Afghan from the large Abdali tribe; he took charge of Nadir Shah's treasury (and the diamond), achieved recognition in Kandahar as tribal leader and proceeded to carve out for himself the largest section of Nadir Shah's territory in a greater Afghanistan that included the Punjab, Sindh, Persian Khorasan and all of modern Afghanistan. He coped with internal opposition, including the rival Ghilzai tribe, and led his army in constant expeditions to maintain his frontiers. His victories over the last Moghuls and the emerging Mahratta confederacy made it easier for the British later to control central India. He and his successors fought the Persians in Khorasan, and the Amir of Bokhara south of the Oxus (who presented him with the cloak purported to have belonged to the prophet Mohammed, which he put in a mosque in Kandahar – waved in public by Mullah Omar). Ahmad Shah changed the name of his tribe to Durrani, the name given to his empire; it was also known as 'the Kingdom of Caubul' after his son had shifted the capital there in 1775. This was the ancestor of today's Afghanistan.

Ahmad Shah Durrani was a respected ruler as well as a good general, but his empire was whittled away after his son and successor Teimur Shah died, and their Saddozai descendants squabbled bitterly among each other. For a time Herat was independent. After a period of confusion and civil war another branch of the Durranis, the Mohammedzais, took over in the person of the Amir Dost Mohammed, who ruled, with interruptions, from 1834 to 1863. (One of the Saddozai princes, in exile, was obliged to give the Koh-i-Noor diamond to the Sikhs, from whom it eventually found its way to the crown of Britain's Queen, and was displayed at the Queen Mother's funeral.)

By now colonial powers had established themselves round the world, thanks to sea power and modern weapons, and in India the British, originally seeking trade but subsequently territory, had eclipsed the Portuguese and French. Through the East India Company they controlled the Bengal, Madras and Bombay Presidencies. At the same time, from the north, Russia, a land colonial power, was overcoming and absorbing the by now decadent Central Asian Turkish khanates, one by one. Political confrontation between the two empires became known as the 'Great Game'. Nervous about reports of Russian agents in Afghanistan, proponents in Delhi of a more 'forward' policy conceived the misguided idea of sending an army to Kabul to put Shah Shuja, a Saddozai prince, on the throne. British lines were extended (Punjab was then ruled by the Sikh state) and the strength of anti-foreign feeling in Afghanistan was gravely underestimated. British envoys were murdered, the aged general in charge was incompetent, and – except for some taken as prisoners – all but one man of the army were massacred in trying to retreat over the high passes to Jalalabad. This was the First Anglo–Afghan War (1838–1842). After the independence of the American colonies it was the expanding British Empire's most traumatic defeat. The British sent a column to burn the Kabul bazaar as a symbolic gesture, but then left, leaving Dost Mohammed once more in charge. Shah Shuja was murdered.

Dost Mohammed's son and successor, the Amir Sher Ali (ruled 1863–1879), was genuinely tempted by Russian blandishments. When the British heard that he had signed a secret treaty with them they invaded, and, when the British embassy was sacked and their ambassador murdered, British armies marched into Kabul from two directions, this time with success (the Second Anglo–Afghan War, 1878–1880). Sher Ali went into exile. The British wisely did not want to stay, and were fortunate to find an ambitious junior relative of the Amir who was ready to take over, while agreeing to keep the Russians at arm's length. Foreign policy was to be conducted through the British.

The Amir Abdur Rahman (ruled 1880–1901) proved to be a strong character, who united and pacified the country by a mixture of persuasion and brute force. It helped that the borders were settled at this time: in the north mainly along the Oxus, with the tongue of the Wakhan Corridor in the north-east deliberately separating Russia from British India, and touching China; in the south the Durand Line divided Afghanistan from India, though it cut through the territories of several tribes and has never been formally accepted by Afghan governments. It enabled Abdur Rahman, however, to take control of certain semi-autonomous peoples who were now clearly within his territory. These included in particular the Hazaras in central Afghanistan and the Nuristanis in what was then known as Kafiristan, since the people were 'non-believers'. Nuristan was invaded from several directions, starting in a winter campaign to prevent the people escaping to the high mountains. There was considerable resistance, however, and a number of people took refuge in Chitral, where they still live alongside the Kalash and have become converts to Islam. The full story of that episode has never been written, certainly not from the Nuristani side.

It was during the reign of Abdur Rahman that the present ethnic distribution of population in Afghanistan took shape. Descendants of the original Indo-European Persian-speaking people, the Tajiks, were concentrated in certain areas, such as Badakhshan and the Panjshir, in the west round Herat, and north of Kabul in the Shomali plain, but Tajiks are to be found everywhere, particularly as craftsmen and shopkeepers in the towns. They were never considered good fighters until Ahmad Shah Masud and his supporters in the Northern Alliance proved the contrary. The Pushtuns (anglicised by the British as 'Pathans') were partly concentrated in their tribal mountain territories on the southern borders, but the two largest tribes were more widely spread: the Durranis all round Kandahar, and the Ghilzais further east round Gardez, south of Kabul. But Abdur Rahman also transported groups of

Pushtuns, who had always been renowned for their martial qualities, to the west and to the north to defend his frontiers – particularly, for example, round Kunduz.

Uzbeks remained in the northern plain round Mazar-i-Sharif, and were joined by a group of Turks with more pronounced oriental physiognomy, who settled north of Shiburghan. These were the Turkomen, many of whom came over from Turkmenistan later, after the Russian Revolution. They brought welcome foreign exchange through their husbanding of Karakul sheep and fine carpet weaving. To complete the Turkic element a few Kirghiz nomads lived in the high Wakhan plateau, and the four Chahar Aimak tribes in the north-west, semi-nomadic, may be a Turkic–Tajik mixture. The educated urban Qizilbash are descended from Turkic military units that had formed part of Nadir Shah's army, and became very influential under the Saddozais. They are Shia and now completely Persian-speaking. Many settled in India, now Pakistan, after the Anglo–Afghan Wars. The Hazara live in the high Hindu Kush around Bamian, but more recently also have settled in parts of Kabul, where they were first employed for manual labour. When attacked by Abdur Rahman many of their leaders took refuge in Quetta, now Pakistan, where their descendants still live. A number of Baluch, mixed with Brahui, live in the Helmand Valley in the south-west.

Finally, the people of Nuristan appear to have had little contact with the outside world over the centuries. They may be relics of some original Indo-European population isolated in the mountains, sharing common cultural values though speaking a number of different languages (see following Annex 2 for theories about their origin).

Abdur Rahman was succeeded by his son Habibullah, who ruled peacefully but was assassinated in 1919. The latter's third son, Amanullah, was in command of the Kabul garrison and seized power, which he consolidated by embarking on a month-long war with British India across the North West Frontier (the Third Anglo–Afghan War). His army made some minor advances, under General Nadir Khan. There were no border changes but the British, weary after World War I, were prompted to restore Afghanistan's autonomy in foreign affairs – i.e. to accept full independence. King Amanullah was a complex personality who saw himself as an Afghan Ataturk, sweeping away medieval customs. After a grand tour of Europe, during which he was feted, he introduced co-education and his wife appeared without a veil. Rumblings of discontent, led by the mullahs, were universal when the King instructed all people in Kabul to wear Western clothes. Eventually a full-scale armed revolt, headed by a Tajik brigand called Bacha Saqao (meaning the 'water carrier'), forced the King and his family to flee. For nine months anarchy reigned.

The successful general in the last Anglo–Afghan War, Nadir Khan, and his brothers of the Musahiban family, descended from a brother of Dost Mohammed, had disassociated themselves from Amanullah because of his hare-brained schemes. They now mobilised tribal forces on the Indian frontier, advanced and took Kabul, executing Bacha Saqao and restoring order. Amanullah remained in exile in Rome. Nadir Shah was proclaimed King and ruled from 1929 to 1933, when the son of a rival with a grudge assassinated him. Unusually for Afghanistan, his brothers did not compete for the throne but supported Nadir's young son, as King Zaher Shah, their constitutional monarch. His uncles Hashem Khan and then Shah Mahmud Khan were Prime Ministers and kept the country neutral in World War II. In 1953 Sardar Daoud, the son of another uncle (who had been murdered in Berlin), became Prime Minister, supported by his brother Naim as Foreign Minister. He was a strong personality and ruled with a firm hand, gradually introducing some modernising reforms and trying to play the Russians off against the Americans to obtain aid from both. His nationalistic policies for a greater Pushtunistan, however, led to a major deterioration in relations with Pakistan.

In 1963 Daoud resigned over differences with other members of the royal family, and for ten years the King took the reins into his own hands. He initiated a proper democratic process (earlier experiments had faltered), which meant that all ethnic groups were for the first time represented in Parliament. There was the beginning of a free press. But political parties were not permitted and the moderate democratic element became squeezed out between competing extreme leftists and Islamicists. Then in 1973, when the King was abroad, Daoud came back from retirement in what could be interpreted as an act of revenge on his cousin and brother-in-law, overthrew the monarchy and government, and declared himself President. This was called the Saur Revolution, after the month in which it occurred. The King became another exile in Rome. In this way Daoud started the process that led to years of disruption and killing in the country. He was able to achieve power only with the help of a number of leftist army officers who had been trained in Russia. At first he appeared to be under their thumb, but as he began to reassert his authority, and to take his former independent nationalist line in foreign policy, hardline Communist elements proved to be too strong for him. In 1978 he and his brother Prince Naim, and many members of their families, were mown down, with their guards (many of whom were Nuristanis), in the palace in a Communist coup. There were mass purges in the country. The Russians may not have planned the coup directly but they welcomed it and took immediate steps to give it support.

The new Communist President, Taraki, did not last long. There was strong rivalry between his co-conspirators. One of his Deputies, Hafizullah Amin, from the Khalqi faction (mostly Pushtu-speaking and rural), was particularly ambitious and ruthless, and soon saw to it that the other Deputy, Babrak Karmal, of the more moderate Parcham faction (mostly Persian-speaking and urban), was posted abroad with other colleagues as ambassadors, then sacked and vilified. They took refuge with the Russians. In 1979 Amin ousted and probably murdered Taraki, who disappeared, but his own unpredictability as an ally eventually persuaded the Russians to move in, at Christmas that same year, and occupy Kabul. Amin was killed and Barbrak Karmal was installed with a puppet government. The world protested, but Soviet control became a fait accompli.

Meanwhile, resistance by different groups of mujahideen with various Islamic credentials developed and spread all over the country, including in Nuristan. Hatred of Russian occupiers fed back through disillusioned Soviet soldiers, to stimulate Glasnost and moderate forces in Moscow. In 1986 Gorbachev, aiming to make the regime in Kabul more acceptable, replaced Karmal with Najibullah, a former head of the Afghan KGB, who put out feelers to non-Communist elements in the country. Even when the Soviet government withdrew its forces in 1989, echoing US experience in Saigon, after a conference sponsored by the United Nations, Najibullah managed to stay in power for a few more years, keeping mujahideen forces at bay. Before a successor, broad-based government could be put together by the UN, however, Najibullah was overthrown in an internal coup, and the vacuum in Kabul was filled by the forces of Masud of the Jamiat party from the north. The Jamiat leader, Burhanuddin Rabbani, became President, a post that was meant to rotate, and when he refused to give it up his former pupil and intense rival, Gulbuddin Hekmatyar, shelled and destroyed much of Kabul. American money and arms, which had played a crucial role in enabling the mujahideen to defeat the Russians, particularly when hand-held Stingers were introduced that could shoot down helicopter gunships, had been channelled through the Pakistanis, and Hekmatyar, a Ghilzai Pushtun born in Kunduz, had been the latter's favourite. With mujahideen fighting each other banditry became rife, and when a new group of Islamicist Pushtuns arrived on the scene in Kandahar, promising a return to strict law and order, they were initially welcomed. These were the Taliban (meaning 'students'), indoctrinated into an extreme form of Islam in religious colleges in Pakistani Baluchistan. They were encouraged by the Pakistanis as a group who could pacify and stabilise the country and make possible oil pipelines to Central Asia. Led by the one-eyed Mullah Omar, they quickly absorbed or defeated other groups, including even Hekmatyar, and took Kabul in 1996, pursuing Rabbani and Masud to a northern enclave. Eventually they controlled over 80% of the country.

We are now in the realm of recent history. The Taliban, ignorant and narrow-minded, were inept at government and gradually became more extreme. They also began to depend financially on the drugs trade and on a maverick Saudi, from a very wealthy family, Osama bin Laden, who had given some assistance to the struggle against the Communists but had more recently become violently hostile to the United States. They allowed him to operate training camps in Afghanistan for terrorists. Among those so trained were the perpetrators of the attack on the twin towers of the World Trade Center in New York on 11 September 2001.

This evil act, in which thousands of innocent people, including Muslims, perished, was falsely purported to be carried out in the name of Islam. It prompted the creation of an international coalition, led by the United States, and including almost all Muslim states, which, with the help of the Northern Alliance (fired by the assassination of their leader

Masud just before 11 September), swept the Taliban from power. The first steps were taken at a conference in Bonn to build a political process leading to a democratic Afghanistan, which the people want, if law and order can be maintained. The King, now an old man, returned to Kabul as 'Father of the Nation'. A Loya Jirga, the traditional national decision-making body representing all elements in the country, confirmed a Pushtun, Hamid Karzai, as the President of the interim government, until elections should be held after two years. Economic assistance was urgently needed. Meanwhile, bin Laden disappeared.

A liberal constitution was agreed by a subsequent Loya Jirga and a largely successful election was held in 2004. Karzai was the clear winner. There had been a surprisingly good turnout, which was a considerable achievement. However, in 2005 bin Laden and Mullah Omar were still at large. US forces were facing some continuing opposition from Taliban elements, especially in the south-west. The new President still needed US special forces for his protection, and several warlords did not yet accept the central government's writ. The invasion of Iraq and its aftermath continued to divert necessary aid and attention away from Afghanistan, and the world was still confronted with the difficult task of trying to eradicate the Al-Qaeda terrorist network.

Annex 2: Origins of the Nuristanis

It will be clear from Barrington's narrative that few of the best-informed Nuristanis that we met seemed to have any real idea of the origin of their people. Kendrick's account of the time confirms this, adding only that the Vakil in Waigel maintained that the people of Wama and Waigel, Aryans originally from Badakhshan, had occupied their present valleys by pushing the Katirs from them. Some people in Wama believed that they were, in contrast, of Arabic origin, and had been forced up into the mountains from the Kunar plain.

The origin of the inhabitants of Nuristan has puzzled their neighbours, and scholars, since ancient times, probably because they were a self-contained, isolated community with a distinctive culture, which was not aboriginal. One of Sir George Robertson's observations about the 'Kafirs', highlighted by the historian Louis Dupree, was that 'their present ideas, and all the associations of their history, are simply bloodshed, assassination and blackmailing; yet they are not savages. Some of them have the heads of philosophers and statesmen.' Within their own communities they were known to be hospitable and good-humoured, enjoying music and dancing. Sir Alexander Burnes was told that the Kafirs 'treat all men as brothers who wear ringlets and drink wine'.

Going back to the earlier records, their love of wine suggested that they might be related to a people called the Nysaens mentioned by Arrian, historian of Alexander the Great, who wrote around 120 AD. He said that these people, who worshipped Bacchus and the vine, lived between the Kabul and Indus rivers. Alexander was delighted with Nysa's traditions and recruited cavalry from that town for his armies. Marco Polo (circa 1270) mentions Muslims addicted to wine living on the northern slopes of the Hindu Kush near modern Nuristan, and a province of 'Pashai' further south containing idolaters with a peculiar language who wear much jewellery.

While Zoroastrianism and Buddhism flourished in regions around them, the Nuristanis kept to their own polytheistic religion, worshipping a pantheon of gods, headed by Imra. Even when Central Asia became converted to a militant Islam, following the incursions of the Arabs and then the Turks, and despite an assault by that world-conqueror Tamerlaine, the Nuristanis, now called 'Kafirs' (meaning 'unbelievers'), retained their own customs and ceremonies. From time to time they began to take pride in descending from their mountain villages to kill Muslims in the plains below.

On the other hand, as 'un-believers' in a prevailing culture in which slavery was accepted, the 'Kafirs' were victims of slave raids, particularly by the Uzbeks in the north. The American adventurer General Josiah Harlan describes this trade, which also affected the Hazaras, in his personal narrative of 1823 to 1841 (see 'Bibliography' annex). The Amir Dost Mohammed proudly showed Alexander Burnes an attractive ten-year-old 'Kafir' boy that he kept among his slaves. The fact that Nuristanis had Aryan features, and many had fair complexions and blond hair, contributed to their attraction as slaves and concubines.

As far as historical references are concerned, Tamerlaine's memoirs merely describe the difficulties of his unsuccessful Nuristan campaign and end with a prayer of thanks for his deliverance from that inhospitable country. The Emperor Babur's very readable memoirs (see 'History' annex above) mention Kafiristan, from where there came a strong and heady wine. He even refers to the Pech Valley as one of the sources of that wine. When he took Chighe Serai, he reports that some Kafirs had helped the local people oppose him. Each had a leather bottle of wine round his neck. The people were 'heathenish' and feared neither God nor man. But these reports give us no opinions on the origins of the Nuristanis.

* * *

When the first British explorers and travellers arrived in the early nineteenth century they found the mysterious 'Kafirs' fascinating, and recorded all sorts of rumours and legends about their origin. Only a few intrepid individuals actually penetrated Nuristan, notably the maverick adventurer Alexander Gardner (in the 1850s). He ended up working for the Sikhs, but left few records. Later, in the 1890s, Sir George Robertson produced his classic book about living with the Kafirs. Most reports were, therefore, second-hand, though often based on talking to Kafirs who had left their homeland for one reason or another.

Mountstuart Elphinstone, British envoy to the Durrani monarch, in his comprehensive work *An Account of the Kingdom of Caubul and its Dependencies* (1815) devoted some ten pages in Appendix C to the 'Caufirs', although he said these did not belong to the King's dominions. He had got only as far as Peshawar, then very much in the heart of the Durrani Empire, but he made extensive enquiries about the Kafirs. He wrote that they 'had many points of character in common with the Greeks. They were celebrated for their beauty and their European complexion, worshiped idols, drank wine in silver cups or vases, used chairs and tables, and spoke a language unknown to their neighbours.' It was reported to him that the people had no name for their own nation, only their different tribes. They counted by scores, not tens. The several languages had some words in common and all had a connection with Sanskrit. He concluded that this derivation of their language 'seems fatal to the descent of the Caufirs from the Greeks', a perceptive opinion in view of later linguistic studies.

The British explorer Lieutenant Alexander Burnes, later Sir Alexander, to be killed in Kabul in 1841, became famous as an expert on Central Asia and travelled widely in Afghanistan and farther north in the 1830s. He wrote a good deal about the Kafirs, whom he considered might be the 'aboriginal' (meaning, possibly, the 'original') people of Afghanistan.

Another inveterate traveller, Charles Masson (1800–1853), was fascinated by Kafiristan. He spoke to several 'Siah Push' young men who had been kidnapped as children. He came to no firm conclusion as to their origin, though, like others educated in the classics at that time, he was attracted to the idea that the fair-haired Kafirs might be descendants of Alexander's soldiers.

Colonel John Biddulph (1840–1921) travelled extensively in Central Asia, and was a coin collector and linguist. In Chitral he found himself near the eastern border of Nuristan and included a chapter in his *Tribes of the Hindoo Koosh* on the Siah Posh, which is worth reading. He mentioned conjecture that the people were of Greek descent, though a Russian he met had claimed they were Slavs! After talking at length to some Siah Posh Kafirs he concluded, however, that that there was little doubt that the Nuristanis were 'a number of Aryan tribes who from the force of circumstances are living now in the same primitive state that they enjoyed long before the commencement of the Christian era'. He wrote that 'there are grounds for supposing that the religion of the Siah Posh is a crude form of ancient Vedic'. The Siah Posh believed that they were descended from one of three brothers, two of whom became Muslims. Their ancestor who refused to do so was called 'Koorshye', which had perhaps persuaded Muslims that they were from the Arab Qureish tribe – a theory that Biddulph said was without foundation.

George Robertson himself, in his extensive writings in the 1890s, related numerous theories about the origins of the Kafirs, which had been given to him by various individuals he had met. There was little consensus. Some claimed Arab ancestry. One man even told him that, at some time in the past, wealthy Kafir notables had separated themselves from the rest and gone to London! Most agreed that the Kafir tribes had once occupied a much larger area, stretching eastwards towards Gilgit. The artisan slaves, who were then a strange feature of Kafir society, were considered to be the remnants of an even more ancient people. No theories were convincing. (According to Klimburg, former slaves, called the 'Bari', are still at the bottom of the social ladder in most villages in Nuristan.)

Robertson concluded that 'the only hope which remains that the Kafirs may be eventually assigned their proper place in the general history of the world is from a comparative study of their language, their manners and customs, and their religious ceremonies, as well as from their cranial measurements, and other other anthropometric observations'. In a telling sentence he wrote: 'Civilisation abruptly fell asleep centuries ago in Kafiristan, and is still dormant.'

Later British writers such as Sir Thomas Holdich, of the Indian Survey, speculated about the Nuristanis, referring to the stories about Nysa in Alexander's time. 'They live their primitive lives,' he wrote, 'enlivened with quaint ceremonies and heathenism equally reminiscent of the mythology of Greece, the ritual of Zoroaster and the beliefs of the Hindu.' He went on to say: 'Who will unravel the secrets of this inhabited outland, which appears at present to be more impracticable to the explorer than either of the poles?'

More recently, Robin Lane Fox, in his book on Alexander the Great, describes how the story of the Kafirs attracted the attention of the Victorian British: 'In the nineteenth century the Kafirs did not yet practise as Hindus or Muslims, so some said they were early Christians un-corrupted by the Catholic Church, others that they were Jews, while others believed that they were Greek descendants of Alexander's garrisons, and hence had a European look, a story which was as old as Marco Polo, and is still repeated.' Fox goes on to say: 'Kipling even paid these proto-Hellenes the honour of a story. But exploration proved that they neither spoke Greek nor cared for Jesus, and their origins soon lost popular appeal...research has discovered...that the Kafirs are descendants of the first invaders to sweep west from India to Europe several thousand years before Alexander.' (South and west into India and Europe would probably be more accurate.) Kipling's short story was, of course, 'The Man Who Would be King'.

Louis Dupree, who studied all aspects of Afghanistan, had this to say in his introductory notes to a reprint of Sir George Robertson's book: 'It is possible that the Kafirs represent the first major explosion (3rd–2nd millennium BC) of the Indo-European speakers from South Russia and Central Asia.'

Almost all writers and historians have accepted the view that the Nuristani people at one time occupied a considerably larger area, and have been pushed back gradually into their high mountain fastnesses.

* * *

Given that the people of Nuristan have no written records (and that there are no rock inscriptions), there are various classic ways of trying to determine their origin:

1. Oral tradition. This is interesting to explore, but, as has been indicated, most stories are vague, and often contradictory. Few

Nuristanis can speak with any authority about their early history, although it is said that some elders can quote many generations of their ancestors.

2. Archaeology. Nothing serious has been attempted so far and there are few promising sites. Wooden buildings may not offer much, and old silver drinking cups are unlikely to have been cast away.

3. Physiognomy. The striking appearance of many Nuristanis, with some 20–30% having blond or reddish hair, has raised many questions, but so far produced few answers.

4. Linguistics. The main line of study has been linguistic: the relationship of the four or five Nuristani languages, which share certain words, to other ancient or modern languages. The pre-eminent scholar in this area – indeed, for all Himalayan languages – was Professor George Morgenstierne of Oslo. He and his successors, such as Professors Buddruss of Mainz and Fussman of Strasbourg have generally concluded that the Nuristani languages are part of the early Indo-Iranian language group, itself part of the Indo-European language family. While some argue that the Nuristani languages belong more to the Iranian or to the Indian side, it is now widely considered, by these authorities, that the Nuristani languages may have developed separately at roughly the same time that the Iranian and Indian strains diverged; i.e. that they comprise a third strain. Morgenstierne himself wrote that 'the Kafirs probably inhabited their secluded valleys since time immemorial, and have never belonged to the community of civilised Indian peoples'. If all this is true, it suggests that the Nuristanis may be a fossilised original Indo-European-speaking people. Max Klimburg inclines to this view. (It is unfashionable now to talk of Aryans, since academic opinion is that the peoples who spoke Indo-European, and, therefore, Indo-Iranian languages, may not necessarily have belonged to the same race.)

5. Genetics. Using DNA, genetics is increasingly being applied to archaeological research. Perhaps work in this latest field will provide definite corroboration of the origins of the Nuristani people.

If it turns out that the Nuristanis are indeed an example of some of the purest early Indo-European stock, this itself will be of tremendous interest. The Amir Abdur Rahman was reputed to have said, 'The Kafirs have been independent for 2000 years and it is I who have reduced them to submission.' The Nuristanis may one day learn to be proud of those 2000 years.

Annex 3: Selected Bibliography

Note: The following bibliography is not meant to be exhaustive, but to cover some of the best-known works. Comprehensive bibliographies are to be found in Max Klimburg's *Kafirs of the Hindu Kush* and Karl Jettmer's *Religions of the Hindu Kush*, Volume I, both listed below. See also Schluyer Jones' annotated Bibliography of Nuristan and his very useful Bibliography of Afghanistan 1992.

NURISTAN/KAFIRISTAN – PRE-1960 WORKS

Arrian, *History of Alexander and Indica* 2 vols, ed. and trans. by E. Iliff Robson, Loeb Classical Library, London, 1929.

Bellew, H.W., *An Inquiry into the Ethnography of Afghanistan*, London, 1891 (reprinted in 1973 by Akademische Druck u. Verlagsanstalt, Graz, Austria).

Biddulph, John (Col.), *Tribes of the Hindoo Koosh*, Calcutta, 1880 (reprinted in 1971, preface by K. Grutzl, by Akademische Druck u. Verlagsanstalt, Graz, Austria).

Burnes, Sir Alexander, *Cabool: Personal Narrative of a Journey to that City*, John Murray, London, 1842 [see chap. 9].

Burnes, Sir Alexander, *Travels into Bokhara*, John Murray, London, 1842 [see Vol. I, chap. 5 and Book I, chap. 3].

Caroe, Sir Olaf K., *The Pathans, 550 BC – AD 1957*, London and New York, 1958 and 1964 (reprinted in Karachi in 1973 and 1986: paperback, 1965).

Elphinstone, Mountstuart, *An Account of the Kingdom of Caubul*, London, 1815; 3rd edn, 2 vols, London, 1839 (reprinted in Graz in 1969; facsimile with introd. by Sir Olaf Caroe in Oxford in 'Asian: Historical Reprints from Pakistan', Karachi, 1972 [Elphinstone's Appendix C has considerable material on the 'Caufirs'].

Fraser-Tytler, W.K., *Afghanistan: A Study of Political Developments in Central and Southern Asia*, London, 1950; 3rd edn, Oxford University Press, Oxford, 1967.

Gardner, Alexander, *The Memoirs of A. Gardner*, ed. by Major Hugh Pearse, William Blackwood, Edinburgh and London, 1898.

Harlan, Josiah, *Central Asia: Personal Narrative of General Josiah Harlan, 1823–41*, ed. by Frank Ross, Luzac and Co., London, 1939.

Holdich, Col. Sir Thomas, *Indian Borderland 1889–1900*, Methuen, London, 1901.

Holdich, Col. Sir Thomas, *The Gates of India*, Macmillan, London, 1910.

Hughes, T.P., *Christian Intelligencer*, 2 vols, Lahore, 1877–1878.

Khan, Sultan Mohammed, *The Life of Abdur Rahman, Amir of Afghanistan*, 2 vols., John Murray, London, 1900 [see Vol. I pages 282–292 for the Amir's justification and description of the conquest of Kafiristan].

Lentz, Wolfgang, *Zeitrechnung in Nuristan und am Pamir*, Abh.d. Preuss. Akad. d. Wiss. Phifhist, 1938 (reprinted in 1939 by Einzelakag), Berlin.

Maraini, Fosco, *Where Four Worlds Meet: Hindukush*, 1959 (reprinted in 1964, and with translation by F. Green, London.

Masson, Charles, *Narrative of Various Journeys in Balochistan, Afghanistan, and the Punjab*, 3 vols, Richard Bentley, London, 1842. Facsimile, with introd. by G. Hambly, 3 vols, 'Oxford in Asia: Historical Reprint from Pakistan', Karachi, 1974; reprinted in 1995 in Graz.

Morgenstierne, Georg, *Report on a Linguistic Mission to Afghanistan*, Inst. For Semmenlignende Kultarforming, Oslo, 1926.

Morgenstierne, Georg, 'Languages of Nuristan and Surrounding Regions', reprinted in *Cultures of the Hindu Kush*, K. Jettmar (ed.), Wiesbaden, 1974.

Newby, Eric, *A Short Walk in the Hindukush*, Collins, London, 1959.

Pazhwak, Abdal-Rahman, *Afghanistan: Review of Political and Cultural History*, Afghan Bureau of Information, London, 1954.

Robertson, Sir George, *The Kafirs of the Hindukush*, Lawrence and Bullen, London, 1896 (reprinted in 1935 in London and New York); in 'Oxford in Asia Historical Reprints from Pakistan', Karachi 1974, 1985).

Robertson, Sir George, *Kafiristan*, Sasor, 1982 [reprint of an undated text of an official 100-page report on all aspects of Kafiristan and its people].

Shakur, M.A. [Curator of the Peshawar Museum], *The Red Kafirs*, The author, Peshawar, 1946.

Thesiger, Wilfred, 'A journey in Nuristan', *The Geographical Journal*, vol. 123, London, 1957 [covers his journey to the Ramgul and Alingar Valleys].

Vigne, G.T., *A Personal Narrative of a Visit to Ghuzni, Kabul and Afghanistan*. George Routledge, London, 1843 [see pages 234–239].

Wilber, Donald N., *Annotated Bibliography of Afghanistan*, 1956; 2nd edn, 'Behavioral Science Bibliographies', New Haven, CT, 1962.

Younghusband, Sir Francis, *Among the Celestials*, John Murray, London, 1898.

Younghusband, Sir Francis, *The Light of Experience*, Constable and Co., London, 1927.

Yule, Sir Henry (translator and editor) *The Book of Ser Marco Polo*, John Murray, London, 3rd edn, 1929 [see pages 153, 164].

NURISTAN/KAFIRISTAN – POST-1960 WORKS

Auboyer, Jeannine, *The Art of Afghanistan*, Paul Hamlyn, Middlesex, UK, 1968 [p. 61 reports on the wooden statues of Nuristan – some illustrated – and what happened to them].

Bashir, Elena and Israr-ud-Din (eds), *Proceedings of the Second International Hindukush Cultural Conference*, Oxford University Press, Karachi, 1996.

Chohan, Amar Singh, *History of Kafiristan (Socio-Economic and Political Conditions of the Kafirs)*, Atlantic Publishers, New Delhi, 1984.

Dupree, Nancy Hatch, *An Historical Guide to Afghanistan*, Afghan Travel Organisation, Kabul, 1971 [chap. 12].

Edelberg, Lennart, *Nuristani Buildings*, Moegard, Aarhus, 1984 [posthumous].

Edelberg, Lennart and Jones, Schuyler, *Nuristan*, Akademische Druck u. Verlagsantalt, Graz, Austria, 1979 [with good pictures].

Fox, Robin Lane, *The Search for Alexander*, Penguin, Harmondsworth, 1980.

Fussman, Gerard, *Atlas Linguistique des parlers Dardes et Kafirs*, 2 vols, Publ. de l'Ecole Francaise de l' Extreme Orient, Paris, 1972.

Fussman, Gerard, 'Quelques ouvrages recents sue les langues et civilizations de l'Hindou-Kouch (1976–1979)', Journal Asiatique, Paris, 1980.

Fussman, Gerard, 'Nouveaux ouvrages sur les langues et civilizations de l'Hindou-Kouch (1980–1982)', *Journal Asiatique*, Paris, 1983.

Gregorian, Vartan, *The Emergence of Modern Afghanistan: Politics of Reform and Modernization 1880–1946*, Stanford University Press, Stamford, CA, 1969.

Griffiths, John Charles, *Afghanistan* [with historical notes by Sir Olaf Caroe], London, Pall Mall, 1967.

Jettmar, Karl, ed. in collaboration with Lennart Edelberg, *Cultures of the Hindu Kush: Selected Papers from the Hindu-Kush Cultural Conference held at Moesgard 1970* (Beitr. zur Sudasien in forsch), Weisbaden, 1974.

Jettmar, Karl, *Die Religionen des Hindu Kush*, Stuttgart, 1975.

Jettmar, Karl, *The Religions of the Hindu Kush*, Vol. I, *The Religion of the Kafirs*, [with contributions by Schuyler Jones, Max Klimburg and Peter Parkes; English translation by Adam Nayyer], Aris and Phillips, Warminster, 1986.

Jones, Schuyler, *An Annotated Bibliography of Nuristan (Kafiristan) and the Kalash Kafirs of Chitral* [Part 1 summarises earlier references, in books and articles to Kafiristan. Part 2 contains *Selected Documents from the Secret and Political Records of the Government of India*, 1885–1900], Det. Kgl. Danske Vidensk Selsk. Hist-filos-Meddel, Copenhagen, 1966–1969.

Jones, Schuyler, *Political Organization of the Kam Kafirs: Preliminary Analysis*, Det. Kgl. Danske Vidensk Selsk. Hist-filos-Meddel, Copenhagen, 1967.

Jones, Schuyler, *Men of Influence in Nuristan: A Study of Social Control and Dispute Settlement in Waigal Valley, Afghanistan*, Seminar Studies in Anthropology, Seminar Press, London, 1974 [includes a useful account of Abdur Rahman's conquest of Nuristan].

Jones, Schuyler, 'Nuristan: Mountain Communities in the Hindu Kush', *Afghan Studies* 1, Moscow, 1978.

Jones, Schuyler, *Afghanistan – World Bibliographical Series*, Clio Press, Oxford, 1992.

Keay, John, *When Men and Mountains Meet*, John Murray, London, 1977 [with chapter on Alexander Gardner].

Klimburg, Max, *The Kafirs of the Hindu Kush: Art and Society of the Weigal and Ashkun Kafirs*, Vols. I and II, Franz Steiner Verlag, Stuttgart, 1999.

Klimburg, Max, 'The Situation in Nuristan', *Central Asian Survey 2001*, 20 (3), 383–390.

Klimburg, Max, 'The Arts and Societies of the Kafirs of the Hindu Kush', *Journal of the Royal Society for Asian Affairs*, London, November 2004.

Levi, Peter, *The Light Garden of the Angel King: Journeys in Afghanistan*, Readers Union, Newton Abbot, 1972 [Part V deals with Nuristan and refers to our trip on p. 189], revised version, Penguin, Harmondsworth, 1984.

Lines, Maureen, *Beyond the Northwest Frontier*, Oxford Illustrated Press, Oxford, 1980 [covers the Kalash people in Pakistan].

Loude, Jean-Yves and Lievre, Vivianne, *Kalash Solstice*, Lokvirsa Publishing House, Islamabad, 1991.

Melabar, Mohammad Alam, 'A Native Account of the Folk History of Kalashum, a Region of Nuristan in Afghanistan', *Afghanistan Quarterly*, Kabul, 1977.

Melabar, Mohammad Alam, 'The Role of Endr in the Mythology of Ancient Nuristan', *Afghanistan Quarterly*, Kabul, 1978.

Schofield, Victoria, *Every Rock, Every Hill: The Plain Tale of the Northwest Frontier in Afghanistan*, Buchan and Enright, London, 1984.

Watkins, Mary Bradley, *Afghanistan: Land in Transition*, Van Nostrand, Princeton, NJ, 1963.

Wilber, Donald N., in collaboration with E.E. Bacon, C.A. Ferguson, etc., *Afghanistan*, Yale University Press, New Haven, CT, 1962; Human Relations Press, New York, 1988.

Wilson, Andrew, *North from Kabul*, George Allen and Unwin, London, 1961.

Wood, M., *In the Footsteps of Alexander the Great: The Journey from Greece to Asia*, BBC Books, London, 1997.

Note: There were, additionally, many journals containing various articles on Nuristan/Kafiristan through the years. For example: *Acta Orientalia*, Copenhagen; *Afghanistan Info*, Neuchatal; *Afghanistan Journal*, Graz; *Afghanistan Quarterly*, Kabul; *Anthropos*, Fribourg; *Asiatische Stadien*, Bern; *Folk*, Copenhagen; *Indo-Iranian Journal*, The Hague; *Journal of Asian Studies*, Ann Arbor, Michigan; *Journal of Afghan Affairs*, Peshawar; *Journal Asiatique*, Paris.

* * *

AFGHANISTAN: OCCUPATION, SOCIOLOGY, RESISTANCE AND THE TALIBAN – POST-1960

Note: Probably the most comprehensive coverage of Afghanistan, including political developments, until 1980 is to be found in Louis Dupree's *Afghanistan*. Many of the following works touch only lightly on Nuristan.

Adamec, Ludwig W., *A Biographical Dictionary of Contemporary Afghanistan*, Akademische Druck u. Verlagsanstalt, Graz, Austria, 1987 [five prominent Nuristanis are mentioned].

Akiner, Shirin (ed.), *Cultural Change and Continuity in Central Asia*, Kegan Paul International, London, 1997.

Arney, George, *Afghanistan*, Mandarin, London, 1990.

Arnold, Anthony, *Afghanistan: Soviet Invasion in Perspective*, Hoover Institution Press, Stanford, CA, 1981.

Baer, Robert, *See No Evil*, Crown Publisher, New York, 2002 [CIA operative in Central Asia and the Middle East].

Bearden, Milt, *Black Tulip: A Novel of War in Afghanistan*, Random House, New York, 1998 [CIA covert operative in Afghanistan].

Bergen, Peter L., *Holy War, Inc: Inside the Secret World of Osama bin Laden*, New York, Free Press, 2001 [CNN analyst].

Bhargava, G.S., *South Asian Security after Afghanistan*, Lexington Books, Lexington, MA, 1983.

Bradsher, Henry, *Afghanistan and the Soviet Union*, Duke University Press, Durham, NC, 1983, 1985.

Cooley, John, *Unholy Wars: Afghanistan, America and International Terrorism*, London and Pluto Press, Sterling, VA, 1999, 2000.

Dupree, Louis, *Afghanistan*, Princeton University Press, Princeton, NJ, 1973, 1980 (reprinted in 1997 by Oxford University Press, Karachi).

Dupree, Louis, *Afghanistan in the 1970s*, ed. with Lynette Albert, Praeger, Special Studies in International Economic Development, New York, 1974.

Dupree, Nancy Hatch, *Seclusion or Service – Will Women have a Role in the Future of Afghanistan?*, Afghan Forum, Inc., New York, 1989.

Elliot, Jason, *An Unexpected Light: Travels in Afghanistan*, Picador, London, 1999.

Gall, Sandy, *Behind Russian Lines: An Afghan Journal*, Sidgwick and Jackson, London, 1983.

Gall, Sandy, *Afghanistan: Agony of a Nation*, Bodley Head, London, 1986.

Girardet, Edward, *Afghanistan: The Soviet War*, Croom Helm, London and St. Martin's Press, New York, 1985.

Goodson, Larry, *Afghanistan's Endless War*, University of Washington Press, Seattle and London, 2000.

Griffin, Michael, *Reaping the Whirlwind (The Taliban Movement)*, Pluto Press, London and Sterling, VA, 2001.

Halliday, Fred, *Islam and the Myth of Confrontation*, I. B. Tauris, London and Sterling, 1996.

Hiro, Dilip, *Islamic Fundamentalism*, Paladin, London, 1988.

Hodson, Peregrine, *Under a Sickle Moon: A Journey through Afghanistan*, Hutchinson, London, 1986 [he visited the Parun Valley].

Hopkirk, Peter, *The Great Game*, John Murray, London, 1990.

Horan, Hume, 'The US and Islam in the Modern World', *Foreign Service Journal*, Washington, February 2002.

Huldt, Bo and Jansson, Erland (eds), *The Tragedy of Afghanistan: Social, Cultural, and Political Impact of the Soviet Invasion*, Swedish Institute of International Affairs, Macmillan, London, 1984 and Croom Helm, London, 1988.

Hyman, Anthony, *Afghanistan under Soviet Domination 1964–83*, Macmillan, London, 1982.

Lewis, Bernard, *Islam and the West*, Oxford University Press, New York and Oxford, 1993.

McMichael, Scott, *Stumbling Bear*, Brassey's, London, 1991.

Male, Beverley, *Revolutionary Afghanistan, A Reappraisal*, Croom Helm, London, 1982.

Marsden, Peter, *Taliban: War, Religion, and the New Order in Afghanistan*, Oxford University Press and Zed Books, Karachi and London; Oxford University, Zed Books, 1998, 1999.

Newell, Nancy Peabody and Richard, *The Struggle for Afghanistan*, Cornell University Press, Ithaca, NY and London, 1981.

Noelle-Karimi, Christine, ed. with Conrad Schetter and Reinhard Schlagintweit, *Afghanistan – A Country Without a State?* [papers of a conference in 2000 – note articles by Klimburg and Schlagintweit], IKO Verlag fur Interkulturelle Kommunikation, Frankfurt and London, 2002.

Nojumi, Neamatollah, *Rise of the Taliban in Afghanistan: Mass Mobilization, Civil War, and the Future of the Region*, Palgrave, New York, 2000.

Rashid, Ahmed, *The Resurgence of Central Asia: Islam or Nationalism?*, Oxford University Press, Zed Books, Karachi and London, 1994.

Rashid, Ahmed, *Taliban, Islam, Oil, and the New Great Game in Central Asia*, I. B. Tauris, London and Yale University Press, New Haven, CT, 2000.

Rashid, Ahmed, *Taliban, Militant Islam, Oil and Fundamentalism in Central Asia*, I.B. Tauris, London and New Haven; Yale Nota Bene and Yale University Press, 2001.

Roy, Olivier, *Islam and Resistance in Afghanistan*, Cambridge University Press, Cambridge, 1986, 1990.

Rubin, Barnett, *The Search for Peace in Afghanistan: From Buffer State to Failed State*, Yale University Press, New Haven, CT and London, 1995.

Rubin, Barnett, *The Fragmentation of Afghanistan. State Formation and Collapse in the International System*, Yale University Press, New Haven and London, 1995.

Ruthven, Malise, *Islam in the World*, Penguin, Harmondsworth, 1984.

Ryan, Nigel, *A Hitch or Two in Afghanistan*, Weidenfeld and Nicolson, London, 1983, [travelling with Sandy Gall].

Shahrani, M. Nazif and Canfield, Robert L., (eds), *Revolutions and Rebellion in Afghanistan: An Anthropological Perspective*, Institute of International Studies, University of California, Berkeley, 1984.

Tapper (now Lindisfarne), Nancy, *Politics, Gender and Marriage in an Afghan Tribal Society*, Cambridge University Press, Cambridge, 1991.

Tapper, Richard (ed.), *The Conflict of Tribe and State in Iran and Afghanistan*, Croom Helm, London, 1983.

Vogelsang, Willem, *The Afghans*, (USA): Blackwell, Oxford and Malden, MA, 2002.

Wolpert, Stanley, *Roots of Confrontation in South Asia: Afghanistan, Pakistan, India and the Superpowers*, Oxford University Press, New York and Oxford, 1982.

Woodward, Kenneth L., 'In the Beginning, There were Holy Books', *Newsweek*, 11 February 2002.

Yuval-Davis, Nira, *Gender and Nation*, Sage, London, 1997.

Biographies of the Authors

REINHARD SCHLAGINTWEIT

Reinhard Schlagintweit, born on 12 March 1928 in Munich, Germany, son of a medical doctor, grew up in Upper Bavaria and Munich. At age 15 he was drafted into the anti-aircraft forces around Munich, but was discharged a year later, a few months before the end of World War II.

He studied law at Munich University between 1945 and 1948. After passing the first state examination he spent eight months in England, most of the time helping out at a small farm in south Devon.

After a brief interlude in a large Munich bank, Reinhard joined the young Foreign Service of the Federal Republic in August 1952. In January 1955 he was assigned to the German embassy in Ankara, Turkey, and in 1958 transferred to Kabul, Afghanistan, where he served until 1961.

Further posts were counsellor at the German embassy in Bangkok, Thailand (1963–1967), and temporary director of the German Information Office in New York (1970/1971). Years in Bonn followed, first at the Government Press and Information Department, then at the Foreign Office's Cultural Department.

From 1976 to 1979 Reinhard served as ambassador to Saudi Arabia. He finished his career in the German Foreign Office with six years as director general, political affairs for Asia, Africa, Latin America and the Middle East. He retired in March 1993.

After leaving the Foreign Service, Reinhard was asked to manage the German Society for Foreign Policy (1993–1998), where he also founded and directed a Middle East experts study group.

In December 1993 he was elected chairman of the German National Committee for UNICEF, an honorary post he still holds.

During his retirement Reinhard has continued to follow developments in the Middle East, an area that had called for his attention during most of his professional life, in particular Iran, Afghanistan and the Israel–Palestine conflict. He is president of the German Iranian Society. As a member of the board of the 'Arbeitgemeinschaft Afghanistan', a group of German-speaking experts involved in different aspects of research concerning Afghanistan, as well as of the 'Mediothek Afghanistan', a group of younger academics, he participated in organising the international conference 'Afghanistan – A Country Without a State?', held in Munich in June 2000. Lakhdar Brahimi, Francis Vendrell, Oliver Roy and Ahmed Rashid were among the speakers.

Reinhard is married to Silvia Neven DuMont. They have two children and several grandchildren.

JOSEPH T. KENDRICK, PhD

Joseph T. Kendrick (JT) was born in 1920 in Pryor, Oklahoma, of Joseph T. (Sr) and Anne (Williams) Kendrick, both of Welsh extraction, although of progenitors of different generations. The Kendricks were some of the first settlers in America, in the 1630s in Virginia, and through the generations had migrated westwards, finally ending in what was the Cherokee Nation of Indian Territory, an area that was later incorporated into the new state of Oklahoma. As such, JT's early days were spent largely among the Cherokee Indians.

After graduating from high school, Kendrick accompanied his mother on a year's visit to relatives in England and Wales, but at the end of the period, while his mother returned to the States, JT, then 18, went on his own for an extended period through the Balkans, North Africa and Portugal before going back home.

After three years of college at the University of Oklahoma, JT went to work for Congressman Wesley E. Disney in Washington, DC, and subsequently as a non-career officer in the Foreign Service of the Department of State. In time, he was assigned to the American Legation in Managua, Nicaragua. World War II broke out shortly after he arrived there, and Nicaragua was declared a 'critical' zone for fear the Japanese would attempt to establish a foothold there on the continent. Kendrick, not released for military service, remained with the Legation in Nicaragua for several years, but was finally assigned to the American embassy in the Soviet Union. Before reaching his new post, however, he was finally released by the Foreign Service to the military. He served as an officer in the US Naval Reserve, first in preparation for operations in the Kuriles, but then reassigned to Russian-language training for duty in Siberia, and, as this tour was completing, the war came to an end; in time he was released back to the Foreign Service. During this tenure in Washington, he completed his BSc at Georgetown University.

His next detail abroad was the establishment of a new consulate in Gdansk, Poland. Although the war was formally over, the Polish guerrillas were in midst of pitched battles with the newly occupying Soviet forces, with the small American consulate team caught in the middle. Once the new consulate was established, however, Kendrick was reassigned to the mission in Moscow, where he carried out largely economic work, but was able to travel extensively, including to the Caucasus – he was one of the first westerners in many years into this region. After some two years in Moscow he made an application for a new programme by the Department of State for advanced training in Russian affairs, but, after being informed that it would be several years before his name would come up, he resigned and went to Columbia University on his own, where he completed his Master's degree and the new Russian area programme, as well as taking examinations for the career Foreign Service.

Back with the Department of State his next assignment was with a new unit in Bad Nauheim and Bad Homburg, Germany, studying (for two years) the Soviet Union's social, economic and political structure through the interrogations of Soviet defectors and émigrés. From 1952 to 1954 he served as special assistant to the consul general in Munich, engaged in psychological warfare against the Soviet Union. This was followed by another four years in the same work in Washington.

At this juncture, Kendrick's concentration shifted from 'psywar' to Central Asia and national security. He was assigned first to a US Army Russian-language school for a year in Oberammergau, Germany, where he focused on Central Asia. At the end of this period he was assigned (two years) as political officer to the American embassy in Kabul, where as part of his work he was able again to travel extensively throughout the country. Probably his most critical assignment during this period was as a member of an emergency detail dispatched by the embassy, in the air attaché's plane, to Kandahar to ensure the safety of the large American colony there, caught in the midst of the riots taking place over the government's edict removing the burqa for Afghan women.

He was next detailed to Paris as deputy political advisor to the Supreme Allied Commander of NATO (SACEUR), where, apart from numerous Allied training exercises in north Norway above the Arctic Circle, he was acting political advisor during the Cuban missile crisis. His next assignment was as political counsellor of the American embassy in Norway for four years, at the end of which he returned to the Department of State. In Washington (five years), he was primarily concerned with inter-agency national security affairs (mainly negotiations with the Soviet Union on a non-proliferation treaty), followed by a detail to the Office of the Joint Chiefs of Staff. (During this period he completed his academic work at George Washington University – work previously started at Columbia University – on his PhD in political science.) At the end of this series of duties he was named dean of the Centre for Area and Country Studies of the Foreign Service Institute, a training wing of the Foreign Service. In 1978 he elected to take retirement from the Department, largely for health reasons.

Kendrick spent two years at his home in Vail, Colorado, regaining his health, and then returned to Washington, where he served as consultant to the Congressional Research Service on a study for the House Foreign Affairs Committee on ways to improve the consultation process between the executive and legislative branches of the government in the formulation of foreign policy, considered a lacuna in the constitution. Notwithstanding several years of study and the conclusions of the study commission, the newly elected Republican administration was not interested in the issue and it was allowed to die without further consideration. In disgust, Kendrick went to the Himalayas, where he trekked and mountain-climbed for several months in the Mt Everest and Kala Patar region.

Back in Washington, he served for several years on the Intelligence Committee Staff, an inter-agency body under the National Security Council, reviewing US foreign policy for certain countries, including Afghanistan. In 1997 he went to Peru for a short period on a personal basis. In 2000/2001 he was a visiting fellow at Cambridge University, England.

Kendrick was married in 1942 to Loreine York (divorced 1954), and in 1956 married Elise Fleager Simpkins (divorced 1977). He has four children: Pamela York, Drew Trotwood (deceased 1970), Juliette Simpkins (MD), and Katherine Mary. He is the author of several political affairs studies, as well as genealogical works on the Kendrick family. Further biographical data are available in *Who's Who in the World – 2001*.

Kendrick retired to his place in Vail in the high Rocky Mountains of Colorado to work on the text of this book. The task was almost complete when he died on 2 January 2003 following an accident.

SIR NICHOLAS BARRINGTON KCMG, CVO

Born in Essex, England, in 1934, Nicholas Barrington went to boarding school and then on to two years' compulsory national service as a 2nd lieutenant in the Royal Artillery. In 1954 he went to Clare College, Cambridge (of which he is now an honorary fellow), to study economics and law. He obtained a first in his finals but spent much time in social and cultural pursuits, including amateur dramatics – an interest he followed in various places around the world.

Successful in the competitive civil service examinations for the Foreign Office, Barrington was designated to learn Persian as a 'hard language'. He spent nine months at the School of Oriental and African Studies in London, and a further nine months' study attached to the British embassy in Tehran, including two months living in Meshed. He then took up the post of oriental secretary in the British embassy in Kabul, where his Persian was useful, from 1959 to 1961. Back in London, he worked on the Scandinavian desk, occupying at the same time a flat at the top of the Foreign Office as one of four 'resident clerks' who took turns in holding the fort out of office hours.

In 1963 Barrington was posted to join the UK delegation to the EEC in Brussels, just before the collapse of the first British negotiations because of De Gaulle's veto. Nevertheless, the UK government had to be kept closely informed of developments in the Community, in order to keep future options open. Reporting on monetary affairs, and on the European Parliament in Strasbourg, were particular responsibilities.

Barrington sailed for Pakistan in 1965, where he was the first secretary political and head of chancery (coordinating role) in the British High Commission. He arrived in Karachi as the 17-day war over Kashmir was erupting in the north, and was soon sent to establish a new permanent office in Rawalpindi, where the action was. After the crisis, when the bulk of the staff moved up from Karachi, he reverted to covering internal political developments, which gave a good opportunity to travel and meet political personalities in that Ayub Khan era. On several occasions he joined others in making weekend visits to Kabul, then a regular holiday option, and re-established contact with some old Afghan friends.

Brought back to London in 1967 Barrington served for a time on the European desk and then as private secretary to the permanent under-secretary of the Commonwealth Office, before being appointed as assistant private secretary to the British Foreign Minister, Michael Stewart, who was also taking over responsibility for Commonwealth affairs. He remained in the same job with Sir Alec Douglas-Home, after the Conservatives won the election. From this vantage point Barrington enjoyed a comprehensive view of the workings of the British government, and the formulation and execution of its foreign policy.

In 1972 he was sent to Tokyo as head of chancery, in a large embassy in a country becoming recognised as an economic superpower. He found Japanese history and culture fascinating, especially their theatre and Zen Buddhism. In 1974 he did temporary duty as Chargé d'Affaires in Hanoi, which involved briefing in Saigon and an interesting journey via Laos. Returning to Tokyo he was primarily responsible for organising the Queen's successful state visit of early 1975, the first to the country by a British monarch. He was made a Commander of the Victorian Order for his pains.

Back in London, Barrington did a tour as head of information policy department, coordinating the presentation of policies overseas, including trade promotion and liaison with the BBC External Services. He was then posted to Cairo as no. 2 in 1978 at an interesting time, which saw President Sadat's visits to Jerusalem and Camp David. He was able to spend a good deal of time visiting medieval Islamic Cairo and ancient Egyptian sites around the country.

In 1981 he was sent to Tehran as head of the British interests section (of the Swedish embassy) and promoted to Minister. US hostages had been released, but it was a tense time, with threats against westerners. Treated as a normal head of mission, Barrington secured the release of some innocent jailed Britons, and promoted British commercial interests, as things settled down. He resumed an old interest in Persian poetry.

After two years, Barrington was sent for six months to New York as supernumerary ambassador attached to the UK mission to help lobbying at the United Nations, and then given the task of coordinator for all arrangements for the first summit meeting of the G7 in London, working with Margaret Thatcher. Once that was successfully completed he became an under-secretary in the Foreign and Commonwealth Office, dealing with consular, visa and nationality issues, and with relations with the British Council, the BBC, the press and parliament.

Barrington was sent, in what turned out to be his last post, as ambassador to Islamabad in 1987 (transmuted to High Commissioner when Pakistan rejoined the Commonwealth in 1989). Besides reporting on Kashmir, internal developments (including the death of President Zia-ul-Haq), drugs, export opportunities, etc., and watching British interests during the Gulf War, Barrington was much preoccupied with Afghan affairs. The British and most other missions were withdrawn from Kabul in 1989, and just before his final departure Barrington was formally accredited to the Rabbani government in Kabul. He had contacts with all the mujahideen leaders, one of whom he had known from his earlier days in Kabul. Sadly, after the UN conference and Soviet withdrawal, these leaders fought among themselves, and caused most of the destruction in Kabul, which Barrington saw on his only visit, in a UN aircraft. Having being made a Commander of the Order of St Michael and St George for his work in Tehran, Barrington was elevated to Knight Commander while in Islamabad.

He retired in 1994, at the statutory age, to live in Cambridge and London. He has been working on a voluntary basis for a number of educational and cultural charities, particularly those linking Britain and Asia, and Christianity and Islam. One major achievement has been securing the funding, in perpetuity, for a new post of lecturer in Islamic Studies in the Cambridge University divinity faculty. He has been an active trustee of the British Empire and Commonwealth Museum in Bristol, which aims to give an objective account of British activities overseas. He is unmarried, but with numerous godchildren.

NOTE ABOUT SANDY GALL

Sandy Gall is a well-known British broadcaster, journalist and author. He was born in Penang, Malaysia, in 1927 and educated in Scotland at Glenalmond and Aberdeen University. He was a foreign correspondent for Reuters from 1953 to 1963, covering Suez (1956), Hungary (1957) and Congo's independence and civil war (1960–1963). He then joined Independent Television News (ITN) from 1963 to 1992, as a foreign correspondent and later newscaster, reporting from Vietnam (1965–1975), Cambodia, China, the Middle East, Africa and Afghanistan. His last two major assignments for ITN were the Gulf War (1991), where he was the first journalist to report from liberated Kuwait, and the fall of Kabul to the mujahideen (1992).

He made three major documentaries on Afghanistan during the Soviet intervention (1979–1989), as well as numerous news reports. He is the author of ten books. *Behind Russian Lines: An Afghan Journal* (1983) and *Afghanistan: Agony of a Nation* (1986) include accounts of travel through Nuristan. He has also written three thrillers: *Gold Scoop* (1997), *Chasing*

Sandy Gall (left) in the Panjshir Valley with his cameraman and, in profile the Mujahideen leader Ahmed Shah Masud.

the Dragon (1979) and *Salang* (1989); a biography of George Adamson, *Lord of the Lions* (1991); and two volumes of memoirs: *Don't Worry about the Money Now* (1983) and *News from the Front* (1994). *The Bushmen of Southern Africa: Slaughter of the Innocent*, was published in 2001.

Sandy Gall is chairman of Sandy Gall's Afghanistan Appeal (SGAA), which he founded in 1983 as a result of his first visit to Afghanistan. SGAA cares for disabled Afghans, mainly mine victims, and children suffering from polio, club foot and cerebral palsy. He was awarded the Sitara-i-Pakistan by President Zia in 1985, the Lawrence of Arabia Memorial Medal by the Prince of Wales in 1987 and the CBE by the Queen in 1988.

He and his wife Eleanor have four children and live in Penshurst, Kent.